Zero to £1 Million

MY STOCK MARKET LESSONS AND TECHNIQUES

By

James Smith

Table of Contents

1. Acknowledgements 4

2. Introduction...5

3. Beginners' Trades 7

4. Starting Trading..13

5. Market Analysis..15

6. Technical Analysis...20

7. Trend-Following 22

8. Profitable Techniques 27

9. Understanding Trends 29

10. Identifying Trades 41

11. Chart Analysis 52

12. Trading Trends 58

13. Darvas' System...72

14. Decision Making..79

15. Things Go Wrong 81

16. Betting Technique..87

17. Trading Credit Cycles...90

18. Uncertainty..93

19. Trader Vic's Advice 97

20. Reading the Market 109

21. In the Jungle 123

22. Trading a Crisis 133

23. This Time it's Different 140

24. The Boom Bust Model..149

25. Market Crashes 154

26. Macro Trading...166

27. Better Forecasting 186

Conclusion...195

One Final Thought...198

Useful trading websites and blogs 206

Legal Disclaimer 208

References 209

1. Acknowledgements

Very little in life is achieved without the kind help and assistance of others, and so in writing this book I owe a debt of gratitude to several people who helped to create this book. I would like to thank Constance Booth, whose input throughout the writing process has been invaluable, and to Lucy Miles for her time and her editing skills. I would also like to thank Mike Boydell from Moneyam.com for allowing the use of Moneyam's excellent charting package in producing many of the graphics in this book.

Finally, I would like to thank Emma Alder, Charlie Hefner and George Carter. Whilst I thoroughly enjoyed writing this book, completing it has been more engaging than I ever imagined, thank you for your patience.

2. Introduction

Learning new skills presents challenges, especially if high standards of competence are sought. For those who wish to become the best, rigorous training and learning is necessary. It can be said that achieving the greatest success requires the acquisition of the greatest amount of experience and insight, that's why those who succeed are often mentored by the best, allowing generations of accumulated insights to be learned quickly. Hence, people wanting to learn something new wisely seek out others with greater expertise. The insights acquired often make the difference between winning and losing, defining the successful person from the rest. It is my aim to take on the role of coach, putting you right alongside me as I take you through the toughest trading experiences I have encountered during the past 25 years. You will to learn about markets and how to trade, learning lessons the easy way that I had to learn the hard way.

The insights gained in the early years of trading that feature in the first few pages of this book, whilst at first may seem less relevant, actually provide critical insights later on. History shows that markets remain untainted by time, and lessons from the earliest parts of this book retain relevance because they inform about the timelessness of markets and that great opportunities recur. It demonstrates that traders who persevere are rewarded with having seen much of what happens in markets before, increasing their ability to recognise opportunities.

This book necessarily focuses on difficult situations because it is the experience gained during these trades that stimulated new learning, change and adaption, as I sought to learn from the writings of the world's best traders and my own experiences. It is hoped that by publishing some of the most insightful moments of trading, including the background to each trade, that readers will learn more than just trading methodologies, they will understand markets and how to trade.

At the heart of this book is the search for trades with the most favourable risk reward ratios, and the methodologies that enable their recognition and exploitation. Again, this involves drawing heavily on the insights of elite traders, with focus not being on what works in theory, but what has been shown to work profitably in practice. The book starts with a quest in search of the best trading system, but once a good trading methodology has been found I soon realised trading is like the ocean, the more you go into it, the deeper it gets. I learn that just having a good trading system is only part of what is necessary for success.

I learnt that decision making is a key skill and the insights I gained and the trades that taught me the valuable lessons feature in this book to highlight what can happen if bad decisions are made, and how to get decisions right more often. The other non-obvious factor that is the cause of several problem trades is position sizing. Position sizing is the art of correctly sizing the trade – several trades in the book highlight how important this is, and how to get it right.

The final sections of the book go beyond this, furnishing the reader with up to date information about central banking, politics and economics to add the finishing touches to a trader's skill set.

3. Beginners' Trades

At 14 years old my only income was from a paper round, but I wanted to be trader. On television I had seen their lifestyle; the adrenaline-fuelled job and the trappings of success. Their world was so far removed from mine that the leap looked unachievable. I doubted that the career guidance officer at my local comprehensive was ever going to be able to get me an internship in the City. So whilst I thought of asking, I never bothered. After all, kids from Worksop just didn't do things like that.

Yet my opportunity to get involved in the markets did occur whilst I was young. The Government announced that the public would be able to invest in the soon-to-be-privatised British Gas. The initial investment amount was small and could be paid in instalments. I begged my parents for some shares as a Christmas present, which I was fortunate enough to receive. I checked the British Gas share price every single day, willing it higher. The economic boom of the 1980's meant stock prices were surging ever higher, but then the market took a turn downwards. I was unperturbed; the market appeared strong and experts were unanimous that this was a blip. But the selling accelerated and traders panicked. The market dropped thunderously and stocks experienced one of their steepest drops in history, the day became known as Black Monday. The market tried to recover, but each time it failed and descended again.

The financial 'experts' pronounced that the stock market would head lower for the foreseeable future, they said sell or face the prospect of further losses. I listened and wanted out, but calculated that after dealing fees I wouldn't be left with much anyway, so I didn't sell, but expected further losses. The stock market then rallied higher. Expecting it to resume plunging, I tempered my optimism, but much to my surprise the market powered even higher.   Soon stock prices reached their previous all-time high. But they didn't stop there. The stock market went on to reach record highs. British Gas shares increased by over 900% in the next 15 years.

The months following the crash of 1987, when the experts had warned about the perils of owning stocks, proved to be one of the best times ever to buy stocks. The experiences around the time of 1987 crash and the ensuing months provided important first market insights for me. I learned that the highly positive investor sentiment that accompanied the market as it motored higher in 1987 was actually a signal for cautiousness. Excited markets with frothy valuations are wobbly and prone to crashes. Likewise, once the market had crashed and valuations had tumbled to attractive levels, investors should view the cautious tone from market 'experts' and the panicked market commentary in the media as excellent contrarian indicators to buy. I knew my first market insights were hazy and shouldn't be regarded as facts. Nevertheless, I had learned my first lesson about how markets behave, and how quickly they can change.

At 16 I had a part-time job in a supermarket which provided funds to start trading. In the coming years I regularly dabbled, mainly following share tips, hoping to be lucky. After a series of disappointments, I realised that tips, whilst often helpful, were never going to make me rich quickly. If I wanted outstanding results they would have to come through my own abilities. Having little knowledge about the market my journey to becoming a successful trader seemed impossible. I didn't know where to start, but through repeated failures and struggles I started to gain insights. Learning through trial and error was tough, especially as my trading funds were small and every lesson the market taught meant losses. Learning through personal experience was going to be a long, slow and expensive process. If I was going to become a successful trader I had to learn quickly, and in a way that wasn't so costly. I then had a lucky break that opened up the doors to my first trading insights that would lead to real success in the markets.

Whilst hunting for tips in the weekend papers I noticed that a new competition called Fantasy Fund Manager would start soon. The competition gave each investor a notional £10 million to invest in stocks. The portfolio which gained the most over the next 10 weeks would win the £100,000 prize. Remarkably, the leading competitors all managed to multiply the value of their portfolios and by the end of the competition the winner had turned his starting amount of £10m into £502m, beating over 10,000 other contestants. The winner was an amateur trader called Jayesh Manek, and the runner up places were filled with other amateur traders. The result sent shock waves through London's investment community. They had been convincingly beaten by amateurs. Some professional traders accused Manek of being lucky. This criticism hurt, and when the Sunday Times ran the competition again Manek relished the opportunity to silence his critics.

The professional City traders hoped for his failure so that they could reclaim their mantle as unchallenged market experts. But from the early weeks it was clear he was no lucky amateur. Manek once again racked up outstanding gains and amazed the investment establishment when he blew away the competition to take first place with other amateur traders filling the runner-up ranks. The accusations that his first victory was lucky were proven hollow and his performance, and that of the other small investors, demonstrated that small investors could make big money and outperform the city professionals.

The competition aroused much interest in the skills of the traders who performed so brilliantly and the Sunday Times responded by publishing a series of interviews with Mr Manek. Obligingly, he shared his investment techniques. Central to his investment methodology were the lessons contained in a book by Jim Slater called 'The Zulu Principle'. He explained that the unusual title of the book had a hidden meaning. It transpired that the author's wife had developed a peculiar fascination with Zulu tribes. Zulu tribes weren't well researched, with only a limited amount of literature on the subject. Within a short time she had become a recognised expert on Zulus. Slater said that small investors needed to embrace this principle and become experts in a particular area of the stock market, so that they would have an advantage. He said investors should research small companies because they are too small for large investors such as pension funds and banks to actively trade. This focus gives a winning edge over the competition as these companies are often mispriced by the market and therefore they have the greatest potential for gains. In addition, it is easier for small companies to grow rapidly, giving large returns to investors.

Manek focused on small companies that were undervalued and had potentially market moving news due imminently, such as a trading update. Such events raised the profile of the stock, putting them onto the radar of major investors. These stocks were likely to jump in value because the release of financial results triggered major investors to notice the shares and buy large volumes of stock. Manek expertly used this simple technique during the Fantasy Fund Manager game. I purchased a copy of the book and read and re-read it, absorbing every detail. Slater advised readers to focus on identifying small growth stocks arguing that investors should focus on these companies because it is the rate that a company can grow its profits and increase its earnings that ultimately determines the value of a share. The book detailed a simple ratio called the Price Earnings Gap (PEG) ratio. The PEG ratio compares the price of a stock to its future earnings growth rate and provides a simple method to evaluate whether a company is cheap or expensive relative to its anticipated growth rate. The ratio gave the investor an idea of the gap between the company's earnings potential and its current valuation. Companies on the stock market are primarily valued by how much each share of the company will earn and investors compare the amount they receive in earnings from a share to the price of the share. The comparison of the price of a share to the amount a share earns gives the Price Earnings Ratio (P/E ratio). So if, for example, a share was priced at £1.00 and was earning 10p per share then the price would be 10 times the earnings, and therefore it would have a P/E ratio of 10.

To calculate the PEG ratio, it is necessary to first calculate the P/E ratio. Then divide the P/E ratio by the percentage rate at which the stock is expected to increase its earning in the coming year. So as an example:

Excellent Stock Ltd is forecast to grow earnings per share at 25% in the next 12 months of trading but trades on a P/E ratio of 12 giving a PEG ratio of 12/25 =0.48

Good Stock Ltd has a P/E ratio of 17 and projected earnings per share growth next year of 15% would have a PEG of 1 (17 / 15 = 1.1). (Data on earnings estimates and analyst upgrades are readily available on the internet for free at yahoo finance/analysts estimates and various other sites). These sites give the current share price, the current P/E ratio and the forecast percentage increase in earnings for the next 12 months. Many of them (such as digitallook.com) also give the PEG ratio. In this instance Excellent Stock Ltd would be preferred to Good Stock Ltd because it has a lower PEG ratio. The lower the PEG ratio the more earnings growth an investor buys with each pound invested, so investors are seeking to identify companies with low PEG ratios. In Slater's opinion the best stocks were small stocks trading on a P/E ratio of less than 20 with growth rates of 20% plus per year. Slater's methodology had additional filters to refine his search. Some of the most important filters are:-

- The Chairman's statement in the company's most recent annual report had to be optimistic;

- The company had to have a record of growing earnings per share and turnover in at least 4 out of the last 5 years. This is intended to avoid cyclical stocks such as house building stocks which have several very good years, but invariably would then have some very bad years when the economy slows;

- Analysts had to have upgraded how much they expected the company to earn. When analysts upgrade earnings forecasts it means that business is improving faster than previously anticipated. If business is exceeding expectations it often means the good news is not factored into the share price and that current estimates are too conservative.

- Slater's preferred companies have an identifiable competitive edge;

- The company had to have strong return on capital employed (over 20%). The mark of a great company is the ability to make large returns on the capital they use. Companies with a strong competitive edge are often identified by a high return on capital employed; and

- No excessive debt burden. He did not invest in companies with high debts.

From the chaos of the market and the lists of thousands of possible investments Slater's book provided a methodology to identify great shares. I purchased a portfolio of stocks focused on small companies that had an average valuation of 18 times earnings per share but which were forecast to grow earnings at 25-50% per year. At that time the economy in the U.K was strong and the stock market was trending higher with small growth stocks roaring ahead. The portfolio performed strongly. The 1990's was a great time to be investing in the market and small growth stocks were especially favoured by the market. But by the late 1990's the market was looking very expensive, so I searched for stocks that were overvalued so that I could profit from a decline in their price.

4. Starting Trading

I identified a company that was both overvalued and in a difficult situation. Discount clothing retailer Matalan Plc was a highly profitable operation which was expanding rapidly, and its stock price had soared over 700% in the preceding years. Aggressively discounting clothing and homewares was a relatively new concept in the U.K and Matalan dominated the market. Despite the company's growth rate slowing to under 15% per annum, Matalan's shares traded at over 30 times the current year's earnings, which, according to Slater's PEG valuation system made the shares significantly overvalued. But there was another more substantial reason why Matalan's stock price could plunge.

Matalan had minimal competition in the discount clothing and home goods markets, but there were signs this would change. Wal-Mart had just taken over Asda supermarkets and was about to bring its aggressive brand of discount retailing to the U.K. The major supermarkets were eyeing Matalan's lucrative market and some announced their intention to enter to compete head-on. Matalan was about to face a blast of intense competition and it seemed certain that Matalan's profits would disappoint. Add to that a racy valuation, and a potent brew of negative factors would cause Matalan's share price to fall a very long way.

Retailers such as Wal-Mart and Tesco were highly successful. Few barriers stood between them and Matalan's lucrative business. I figured that the U.K market was the same as the U.S market 30 years ago, when a few discounters had grown rapidly and then a plethora of copycats sprang up, causing profits across the sector to fall sharply. For some unknown reason the market wasn't overly concerned that this would happen, and Matalan shares maintained their expensive price tag. This made Matalan a good stock to sell short to profit from the tumbling share price when the market awoke to the emergent threat from new competitors. I had strong expectations of a highly profitable trade, so opened a new short position on £32,000 worth of stock. After briefly falling, the price of Matalan's stock started to increase. Losses mounted sharply until the pain became intolerable and I closed the trade. I suffered nasty losses of over £5000 in a matter of only a few weeks.

Shortly after exiting the trade, Matalan's stock price changed direction, beginning to fall. Then Matalan issued disappointing sales numbers, citing increased competition. Matalan's stock price began melting, losing 80% of its value as the new competitors ate in. It was a painful lesson about stock markets and leveraged trading. Too large a trade had meant it wasn't possible to sustain the position against even a modest move in the market. Instead of a large profit I had incurred hurtful losses, yet I had been right about almost every aspect of the trade. When trading, not only does the analysis have to be correct, but the trade has to also be well timed and of an optimal size. There were no marks for being smart and spotting the deficiencies of a company before the market was ready to acknowledge it. On the contrary, money had been lost for being too early.

Trading proved tough. But, whilst I had lost money on this occasion it was exciting how close I had come to making serious money. My mistakes were those that any beginner could have made. The tuition fee for my errors had been large, but I had come within touching distance of earning big money. A bit more skill and it would be within reach, or so I believed......

5. Market Analysis

The stock market boomed higher as the year 2000 approached. Internet stocks led the market higher, but their valuations were incomprehensibly expensive, with many having multi-billion pound valuations, despite having never earned a profit. In such an expensive market Slater's investment formula wasn't useful in identifying quality investment opportunities because nothing was signalled as being good value, leaving my trusted stock buying system ineffective.

Despite sky-high stock valuations, the media and the general public were giddy with excitement about the prospects for the market. The market rekindled memories of 1987, when it had last exhibited this level of frothiness. It had then crashed and I began to suspect that we sat on the cusp of another market crash; the similarities were startling. In anticipation I quickly sold everything. But the market didn't fall; it rose! Then it increased more, and more, and more!

To highlight my failed judgement a work colleague had followed a newspaper tip to buy an internet stock. He'd enjoyed a tenfold increase in the value of his investment in just 18 months, earning him huge profits. When I considered my own investment performance over the past 12 months I knew that I would have also earned handsome profits if I hadn't followed that darn Jim Slater's book with its focus on company earnings and profitability. His methodology had kept me from one of the most exciting and profitable markets. The feelings of frustration at missing such great opportunities repeatedly filled my mind, especially since other traders were earning fortunes. Yet, whenever I seriously considered how to trade the market, I still reasoned that Slater's system of picking stocks had to be superior to buying stocks without regard for valuation, as many traders who were currently earning big money were doing. Internet stocks couldn't carry on rising indefinitely unless they earned increasing profits, that was for certain.

The more I assessed the business prospects for internet based companies the stronger my conviction grew that the future profitability of internet companies would disappoint. One stock that appeared grossly overvalued was Freeserve Plc. The company provided internet access to households. Customers could easily change Internet Service Providers and therefore the business would always be intensely competitive, with low profit margins. Freeserve was losing money at an alarming rate. Amazingly, when the company released results the stock price leapt higher, with the market looking through eye watering losses to a future that it believed would be extremely bright. It was undeniable that competitive pressure in Freeserve's market was growing, with a plethora of new competitors being launched each month, yet amazingly the stock market still valued the company at £2.6bn. The market put such a high value on each new user that an Internet Service Provider could gain that some companies, in a desperate effort to increase users, promised to pay new customers every time they used the internet. Their rationale was to make money by increasing customer numbers and then float the business on the stock market, thereby capitalising on the market's frothy valuations.

Given the gross overvaluation, trades to profit from a fall in Freeserve's stock price looked to be an outstanding opportunity. I didn't want too large a trade as I needed to be able to hold the trade even if the price moved against me in the short term. All that had to be done was to keep the trade size modest and allow the market time to deflate to more realistic valuations. For the next few weeks Freeserve's stock trended higher in a booming market. Then it fell, along with the rest of the market. With the lesson of avoiding a too large-sized trade at the forefront of my thinking I opened new short positions. The market slide grew. I checked the share price hourly, watching profits fruit as the panic grew and the market slid lower. It wasn't long before the account was filled with the healthy glow of large profits, which I couldn't refrain from watching grow. Yet, just when the market commentary in the media took on a worrisome tone the market stopped falling and reversed. Within a short space of time internet stocks were smashing their way to new all-time highs with a renewed energy and vigour that was inconceivable just days previously.

Profits were displaced by growing losses. The days passed slowly as the market rallied and losses grew. The mounting losses caused me to re-think whether this was a trading plan to doggedly cling on to. I then saw the flaw at the heart of the trade. Its success depended on internet stocks ceasing their prior meteoric rise, but with the sector having already risen by more than was justified by rational judgement nobody could know how high the market would bid these stocks. Even with a modestly sized position I questioned if I could hold out if the price doubled, with the potentiality of yet more increases following. It flashed across my mind that several years ago I had analysed internet stocks and concluded that they were so grossly overvalued that further price appreciation was unlikely, but since then many had multiplied in value.

Flustered, I ran some quick calculations and soon learned more about the dangers of short trades. I realised that short trades exposed the trader to a much higher degree of risk than long positions. For example, if I opened a long trade that £10,000 worth of shares would increase in value, but was horribly wrong, my losses were restricted to the value of my original investment of £10,000. But, if I bet that £10,000 worth of shares would fall in value and got the bet horribly wrong and the stock price tripled, I would lose £20,000. If the price increased six times in value, I would lose £50,000. In fact, because of how high prices can rise, potential losses were unlimited. I knew that the history of markets was full of instances of manias, panics and crashes, but I had never been against the full power of a booming market.

When I had watched the earlier phases of this stock market bubble grow it seemed a benign exuberance. But now, with trades positioned against the market I was feeling its full power. The frenzied crowd of buyers were driving the market higher, and I felt like the one person in the world trying to push back. Every time they pushed the market higher my losses grew, eating away at my trading funds and dissolving my confidence. My resolve to hold onto the trade weakened and the pressure mounted to exit. I noticed that the media pundits had changed tack and they were now talking as though they had never doubted the market's strength. They could change tack effortlessly, whereas I had ballooning losses and a critical decision to make as to whether to jettison the trade.   I decided I'd had enough sleepless nights. If I closed the positions the losses would stop growing, yet the hope that tomorrow would be the day the market would start a decisive turn lower made me hesitate. Eventually I decided that the uncertainty of the growing losses outweighed the joy that even large profits could bring. I closed the trades quickly, whilst trying not to see the large losses that were now without hope of reversal.

Knowing how much I had lost would provide valuable feedback, but I wasn't yet prepared to see the full impact of my mistake. I estimated the losses on a scrap of paper and was disappointed at my failings. Yet, shortly afterwards an unexpected sense of relief blossomed. My happiness was no longer influenced by the latest stock quotation, and I was no longer stressed trying to figure out what the stock market would do next; it felt great to be free. The next few weeks saw the market surge higher, led by internet stocks. The losses would have been horrendous had I not closed the trades.

I had learned an expensive lesson, never to bet against a stock market boom, and drew some consolation that many people had made similar mistakes and paid a far higher price. I was a beginner; I had to accept mistakes, but the important thing was to learn from them, and to keep losses small. Some hard-earned market lessons had been gained. I had sold short shares in a market I thought would move lower. When the market showed me to be wrong I had exited – maybe not as quickly as I should have done, but I'd learnt from that. The stock I had shorted was grossly overvalued by any established investment metric and I now knew that valuation alone isn't a sufficient ground to enter into short positions because markets can become very irrational. Well-positioned stop losses were an absolutely essential pre-requisite for any trade; they had to feature in all future trades if success was ever going to be attained.

Thereafter, the stock market bubble burst and internet stocks crashed. I entered some short trades, but caution prevented any large trades from being executed. I had been taught by the market, in the rudest terms possible, that I was a beginner and there was much I didn't know about trading. My mantra became 'I don't know what I don't know'. This kept me from repeating my earlier mistakes of leaping into the market believing that I was a great trader. I was a novice, and I knew it. Maybe that was my biggest lesson so far.

I studied the market as it headed lower. Some aspects of market behaviour increasingly perplexed me. Why did internet stocks now plunge when they announced increased losses, whereas previously the price had surged higher? What had caused the market to change direction? And was it possible to identify market turning points, because if markets could be irrational, then surely it had to be unwise to use rational judgement to predict the market?

There was much learning to be done.

6. Technical Analysis

Reading trading books and blogs provided theoretical knowledge, with practical experience being gained by testing the ideas in the market. I needed to continue the cycle of learning and testing, regularly checking through online book shops to identify new reading material and then assessing its effectiveness. Amongst the many books I read, one titled 'Market Wizards: Interviews with Top Traders' by Jack D. Schwager proved especially insightful. The book contained transcripts of interviews with elite traders answering questions about their trading methodologies. The traders were also asked about their most notable trades and trading experiences, expressing their opinions about their preferred trading techniques, and what their opinions were on a range of trading methodologies.

Most of the traders interviewed in the book said they analysed markets using both technical analysis and fundamental analysis. Thus far, my focus has been on using fundamental analysis, with Slater's system providing the primary building blocks for a system of identifying stocks to trade. Trading a stock based on the quality of the company and how much it earned always seemed like a logical approach to selecting stocks. In comparison, technical analysis relied on studying the previous price of a stock to make predictions. This never seemed a logical methodology for trading. In fact, it seemed quite bizarre, so I hadn't investigated technical analysis in any detail. However, having just read that elite traders thought technical analysis was at least as significant as fundamental analysis provided a sound reason for further investigation. I was particularly interested in an aspect of technical analysis called trend-following.   This strand of technical analysis was most frequently mentioned by the elite traders. Indeed, several said that they had no regard for any other information when trading, their sole focus was trend-following. I figured if these traders could be so successful without any regard to fundamental analysis then trend-following had to be worthy of further investigation.

7. Trend-Following

Trend-following is a strategy which necessitates that traders always trade in the direction of the prevailing price trend. If a market is trending higher investors should bet that the market will continue in that direction. An elite trader once wrote that he would place the price chart of the market he was thinking about trading on the floor, stand on his desk and look at the chart. If he couldn't determine the direction the price was heading, then the trend wasn't clear and he wouldn't invest (I still think of this principle whenever trading).

This account of such a simple investment technique triggered a reflection on my own trading experiences to assess its validity. I'd lost money on every trade that was against the trend. But when the market crashed I had shorted internet stocks to profit from the trend towards lower prices. Those trades had a very high success rate and I reasoned that if I could identify trends I might catch all the major moves that occurred, and the probability of being caught on the wrong side of a major move in the market would be much lower.

Eager to find out more about technical analysis, I searched for more books. My next purchase was a hefty tome by Edwards and Magee which had received good reviews. At over 600 pages this book was a favourite among hard core technical analysts. On seeing the enormity of the book I realised that technical analysis was an extensive subject. I wasn't disheartened. In fact, I was excited about how much I would learn from such a large book filled with hitherto unknown guidance.

The first section of book focused on an idea called Dow Theory, a relatively simple theory which intuitively made sense. A key aspect of the theory was that when the stock market hits a new high in price the transportation sector should also make a new high. This was logical because if transportation businesses were doing well then the economy must be doing well, since the majority of the goods produced in the economy require transportation. I had personal experience which verified the validity of this observation. During the final stages of the bubble in technology stocks in 2001, share prices in most sectors of the stock market outside of the technology sector were falling. All of the market's price appreciation became focused on a narrow group of stocks. From trading at the 2000 level in June 2000 the NASDAQ increased in value by 60%. Meanwhile the Dow Jones slid from 12,000 to 10,000, with transportation stocks being one of the weakest sectors. The high-flying NASDAQ soon collapsed, losing over 75% of its value in the next 18 months. Knowing caution is warranted when the bull market is led by a small group of stocks was certainly a lesson worth knowing.

The book then proceeded onto the subject of chart patterns. Patterns are given names corresponding to their shape, such as right angled triangles, broadening triangles, symmetrical triangles, ascending wedges, descending wedges, pennants, broadening wedges, to name but a few.

I spent many months learning the definitions for each chart pattern and studying their occurrence. I then searched through the charts of stocks and world markets seeking to identify the best examples of each pattern for opportunities to use my new found knowledge. Where I found the best examples of each of the patterns I would open trades based on the shapes that appeared on the charts. At first I was unsuccessful, but I believed that I would have to persevere so that I could perfect identifying the best opportunities. I traded a wide variety of the shapes that were mention as providing trading signals. Overall, the trading results that I achieved using these chart patterns were abysmal. On further study, I realised that almost any series of prices could be classified as one type of chart pattern or another. I also noticed that one chart pattern could develop into a different chart pattern when the price data from more trading sessions was added.

Figure 1: *Showing a Price Chart with patterns similar to those detailed in Edwards and Magee. 1, Diamond formation. 2, Triangle formation. 3, Ascending wedge.*

After many months of losses caused by trading price patterns I concluded that it wasn't my ability to interpret chart patterns that was to blame, but that most had absolutely no predictive power, they were just random patterns. The methodology was so deeply flawed as to be without use.

I was amazed at why so much literature had been written under the guise of 'analysis' when it didn't offer any trading insights. Investigation revealed that in 1930, Richard Schabacker, editor of *Forbes*, wrote a book called "Stock Market Theory and Practice" which discussed chart patterns. During the stock market boom of the 1920's, when most stocks ran up in a climatic frenzy and then crashed back down again he had concluded that these patterns were predictive of the trend continuing. However, during the 1920's the trends in the market were so strong that almost any period of sideways movement was merely a pause before the market moved onwards in the direction of the price trend. Therefore, classifying the many different price patterns that frequently occurred as indicating that the price momentum would continue wasn't misguided if conclusions were drawn from looking only at the markets of the 1920's. But the market action of the 1920's was abnormal, and inferences should not have been drawn about the predictive qualities of these price patterns in markets of the future. However, books continued to feature these patterns because a threshold had been passed, and identifying these patterns had become accepted as a valid method of analysis. Books which didn't include them were regarded as incomplete. The custom for inclusion continues to the present day.

In more recent times a focused study[1] examining each individual chart pattern was conducted and confirmed that the predictive power of almost all of the shapes that technical analysis identifies as being meaningful chart patterns do not signal good trading opportunities. Despite this, books continue to be published that faithfully recite disproven ideas and fail to differentiate between the aspects of technical analysis that give a trading advantage, and those which don't.

A further problem has been identified with using pattern analysis as the basis for trading. People have a tendency to see patterns even if they aren't present. As an example, if we came home and the front door was ajar and several items were strewn on the floor and the television was gone and we hear noises coming from upstairs we immediately believe that we know what may have happened because our brain inserts missing pieces of information to fill the voids. This instinct helps us survive in the real world, for it is better to wrongly assume that we are in a dangerous situation than to wait until we have all the evidence about the situation, since waiting could endanger us. When trading, subconscious parts of the brain can perform a similar trick and insert missing information, leading us to reach false conclusions.

The ability of our brains to do this is demonstrated by the experiments of Swiss psychiatrist, Herman Rorschach. He dropped spots of ink onto paper and folded the paper to create symmetrical inkblots on each side of the fold. He then asked people to describe what they saw. People described seeing insects, shapes, faces, buildings etc. The conclusion from the experiment was that people saw whatever was on their mind i.e. they projected their thoughts onto the ink marks. The implication for traders is that they are likely to look at random movements of the market yet believe that they have identified meaningful signals about the market's future direction which confirm their existing belief, when really only a random pattern is present.

8. Profitable Techniques

After much more study and many experimental trades using various technical analysis methodologies I knew that trend-following worked, but that many of the other trading approaches coming under the umbrella of technical analysis were less useful. Most offered no useful insights whatsoever! Furthermore, it became apparent that using less reliable indicators in conjunction with trend-following did not add to trading performance, instead the 'noise' generated by the additional indicators detracted from the more reliable signals and diminished trading performance.

The more I studied price trends the more I understood why they occur and why a successful trading system can be built around them. Typically stock prices move in step with company earnings and this was the basis for Slater's stock picking system. It also became apparent that the earnings of most companies bore a significant correlation to the performance of the economy. During an economic expansion stock prices normally trend higher as economic growth increases company profits. Once the economic cycle peaks and the economy ceases to expand, earnings growth slows and the stock market, on anticipating the onset of recession and declining earnings, will typically commence a new trend lower. Therefore, the market price and the trend is an amalgamation of a huge amount of information, making it a valuable trading signal.

Sometimes new trends arise because of factors other than economic fluctuations. The history of the stock market confirms that technological innovations produce exciting new companies. These stocks often trend higher for many years, delivering stellar gains for investors. In an earlier chapter I mentioned the huge gains made by investors in internet stocks, but this wasn't the first occasion that large gains were obtained by investors in stocks at the forefront of a technological era. Investors who owned railway stocks when they were at the vanguard of travel, or aerospace stocks when commercial jet travel became viable earned huge returns, as did investors in radio and television stocks when these technologies were pioneered. History shouts loudly that investors in each era are offered their own unique selection of stocks which trend powerfully higher in tune with booming demand for the new technologies, offering astute traders the opportunity to earn very large returns.

9. Understanding Trends

Price charts can be used to analyse any market; the market's price is formed from the confluence of different factors. It is beyond the comprehension of any individual to know all of the reasons why participants in a particular market are buying or selling, or the price others are prepared to trade at. Fortunately, the market price amalgamates this information. A longer term price chart containing information about how the price has traded over many years contains even more information, and provides invaluable insights into where traders are likely to buy or sell in the future.

A market that is trending higher tells us that buyers are growing in confidence and that this market is worthy of investigation with a view to also buying. Likewise, a new downtrend provides a clear warning signal that the market has changed and new factors may have triggered selling. Examining charts is akin to a doctor examining a patient's electrocardiogram – it conveys information about the strength and pulse of the market, enabling the experienced chart reader to quickly understand the opportunities or threats of a market.

9.1 Understanding Markets

Before progressing we need to understand market prices, and why they change. Markets are influenced by the power of the buyers and sellers. But the reason behind why prices change is more subtle. Large buyers, such as those trading on behalf of pension funds have tremendous amounts of money. They influence the market, pushing it higher or lower with a force equivalent to thousands of small investors. But it is not only the monetary firepower of each investor that determines how the market moves, but also their confidence.

As an example, consider a stock that is trading at £1.00. Let's say that the buyers in the market believe that at most the stock is worth £1.20. If the buyers only believe that the stock is worth £1.20 then regardless of how numerous or powerful the buyers are the price will never rise above £1.20, because none will buy above that price. We would therefore expect the stock to trade at a price close to the £1.20 level, but not above. Let's say some new buyers enter the market, they believe the stock is worth £1.40. The confidence and power of the new buyers is sufficient to cause the price to rise above £1.20 towards £1.40. As the price approaches £1.40 the buying interest would be expected to abate and the traders who believe that the share is worth less will sell, exerting pressure and pushing the price lower again, towards £1.20.

Now let's say that the company issues better news than the market anticipated. Traders raise their estimates of the stock's value, with most now believing the stock is worth £1.60. We would now expect to see a surge in the number of shares traded as people buy the stock, and for the share price to rise strongly. Furthermore, we would expect the stock on that trading day to finish the trading day near to the highest level of the session as it rises back towards £1.60. Therefore, by examining the strength of the price rise and whether it is sustained, along with the number of shares traded we can gain insights into the underlying market. The price chart of the market can inform us about the beliefs of traders in the market. When a rising price encounters selling that is sufficient to halt the advance of the price, this is called resistance. We know that at points of resistance buying interest is weak and traders are less confident about the share price rising further. Where buying occurs that halts a falling price, this is called support. Few sellers are willing to sell below this price level and buying interest is stronger, thus the price fall is abated at support levels.

We see in figure 2 on the following page that when the share price reaches 700-705p sellers enter the market. Their selling prevents further price increases. Likewise, when the price dips to 655-665p buyers enter the market and the buying is sufficient to arrest the price decline.

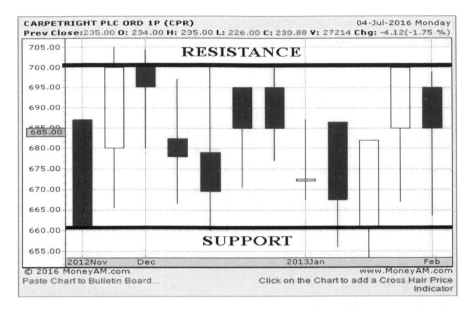

Fig 2. *Support and Resistance points*

Investor confidence is essential for a strong market. Anyone who understands team sports such as football will be aware that key moments often alter the rest of the game because the psychology of the teams is altered. The same occurs in markets. Strength and confidence draws in other investors and can tip the balance of the market, causing new trends. Trends exhibit self-perpetuating and self-reinforcing characteristics. Trends frequently last for many years and often take markets to extreme valuations.

9.2 Uptrends

An uptrend is a series of successive rallies that penetrate the previous high points, interrupted by sell-offs which terminate above the low points of the preceding sell-off, giving the trend line the appearance of the blade of a saw.

Uptrends are a buy signal because they indicate increasing optimism. Rising prices generates investor interest and draws investment into the sector. In turn, this generates media attention which then attracts more investors. The more prices rise, the greater the amount of attention the sector will receive, causing investment in the sector to increase further.

Figure 3. *Example of a Stock in an Uptrend.*

Trends offer advantages other than simply informing us about the balance of the market. Identifying a change of trend direction provides important trading signals, such as when to buy or sell.

Figure 4. *An Uptrend Failing.*

We see in figure 4 an uptrend fails, signalling to sell. The stock trends higher until February 2011, with the price making a succession of higher highs and higher lows. Then the uptrend falters because support at points 1 and 2 fails and the stock falls to new lows at point 3, signalling the trend has ended because it no longer makes a succession of higher highs and higher lows that define an uptrend.

It tells us that buying interest has weakened because it is no longer sufficient to sustain the uptrend. Between point 1 and point 3 additional evidence emerges that the market is weakening when the stock price tries to move higher but fails to exceed the old highs. During this period the price twice attempted to rise, but on each occasion it was met by sufficient selling to satisfy the buying interest.

This example demonstrates that not only can price provide a great signal to buy, but also signals weakness, and when to sell. Using price as an indicator provides an uncomplicated indication of the market's health, giving an early signal that a large move may occur.

Within uptrends the market often forms trading ranges. If the buying interest strengthens the price will break above resistance and exit the trading range to the upside. This is called a bullish trading range breakout. When seen on a price chart this signals that the buyers are strong, indicating that the market will continue higher.

Traders should buy when a bullish trading range breakout occurs. This is because it tells us that the supply of stock at resistance is exhausted. This could be because sellers realise that prospects are improving and they are therefore unwilling to sell. If no more stock is available the price will rise until new selling pressure emerges to satisfy the buying interest, or the buyers are unwilling to pay the price demanded by sellers and cease buying.

Bullish trading range breakouts should only be traded during bull markets when the direction of most stocks is higher as this significantly reduces the number of false signals to buy.

When the price band which defines the support and resistance of a trading range is wide trading is more challenging and is often best avoided because concise signals cannot be obtained about when the price has broken out from the trading range. Figure 5 (next page) shows a breakout from a bullish trading range as the price breaks above resistance at 2050-2100.

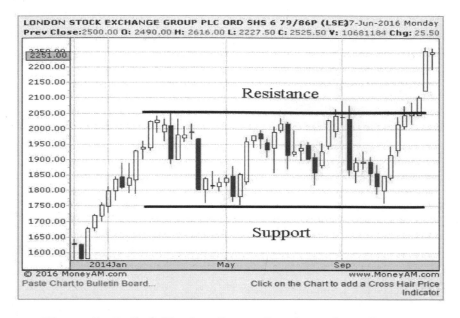

Figure 5. *Bullish Trading Range Breakout above Resistance.*

9.3 Narrow Trading Range Breakout

A narrow trading range breakout occurs when the stock trades within a price band of 10% or less for at least 4 weeks. The narrower the trading range that forms, and the longer time the stock trades within the range, the more significant the breakout is. Narrow trading ranges offer superior trading opportunities to wide trading ranges because tighter stop loss points can be set, giving a better risk reward / ratio. That's because, in a narrow trading range, less distance exists between the price breakout point and the level below where support exists (which is the optimal level to position the stop loss). If the breakout from a narrow trading range fails, key support is breached sooner, signalling the trade should be closed, meaning smaller losses.

When a market rises strongly, and then forms a narrow trading range, the market is signalling that profit taking and other selling pressure cannot push the market substantially lower. We comprehend that potential sellers can only be induced to sell at a price close to the highest recent price and from this we can infer that they are not keen to dispose of the stock because they believe the stock has good prospects.

Fig 6. *Breakouts from Narrow Trading Ranges, 1 and 2.*

9.4 Chart Analysis – St Ives Plc

In figure 6 the share price rises strongly in January 2013. Profit takers move in at 125p and the share price retreats. The price then forms a narrow trading range (box 1). Buyers and sellers are equally matched during this period. It isn't long before the supply of stock at this price is exhausted and buyers express willingness to pay significantly more for the stock, causing the price to break out from box 1 and rise strongly. The ascent ends and the share price trades in a narrow range (box 2). Buyers again demonstrate their keenness to acquire the stock, buying stock close to the recent high in price. The available stock is quickly absorbed and the price rises strongly again.

9.5 Downtrends

A downtrend conveys that the outlook for the market is deteriorating. Never invest in a market that is in a downtrend. Only open trades to profit from the falling price i.e. short trades.

When trading downtrends it is normally best to wait until after a significant rally or the occurrence of a downside breakout from a trading range before opening new short positions because sharp rallies are common in falling markets. These sharp rallies squeeze traders holding short positions, inflicting hurtful losses, pressuring them to buy stock to close their trades.

Figure 7. *Tullow Oil – A Stock in a Downtrend.*

In a downtrend the sequence of lower lows and lower highs is apparent. The chart pattern resembles a cross section through a flight of stairs.

9.6 Bear Trading Range Breakout

Trading ranges often form within downtrends. They occur when the buying interest is sufficient to halt the decline for a substantial period. However, once the buying interest is exhausted the price will drop out of the bottom of the trading range. The price will fall until sufficient new buying interest is aroused, or the price reaches such a low level that sellers no longer offer their stock for sale, believing it to be worth more.

Short trades should be entered when the stock price breaks below the floor of the trading range. In Figure 8 short positions should be entered when SSE Plc's share price falls below 1540.

Figure 8. *Bear Trading Range Breakout.*

9.7 Relative Strength

With many thousands of potential investments available in global markets traders can be very selective about which markets they are active in. To refine selection criteria further we can use another very important indicator called relative strength. Markets signal strength by increasing in value more quickly than less favoured assets. Assets which rise strongly in the initial phases of the bull market have a very high probability of continuing to outperform. Numerous studies have shown that outperformance in the early stages of a bull market is an excellent signal that these stocks will continue to outperform, such stocks are said to have a high relative strength.

History informs that prior relative strength is a potent indicator of future outperformance. From the early 1960's to 2005 the average relative strength of the best performing stocks prior to them making a very large increase in value was 85 (meaning the best stocks to buy were those that had previously outperformed 85% of other stocks). The lesson from this study is that during bull markets stocks which demonstrate impressive strength should be bought and that traders must focus on buying the strongest 15% of the market. Likewise, during bear markets the weakest 15% of stocks should be targeted for short positions, as these are likely to continue falling by the greatest amount.

Relative strength is determined by comparing the price performance of stocks. In a basket of 100 stocks the best performing stock per year has a relative strength of 100, the second best 99, the third best 98 etc. Most charting packages have the ability to provide a comparison of the price performance of multiple stocks enabling traders to assess relative strength.

Figure 9 on the following page shows a comparison of relative strength using a share price chart to highlight the difference in relative strength between two stocks. Most free charting packages enable comparison between multiple stocks enabling a trader to quickly and easily identify the stock with the highest relative strength.

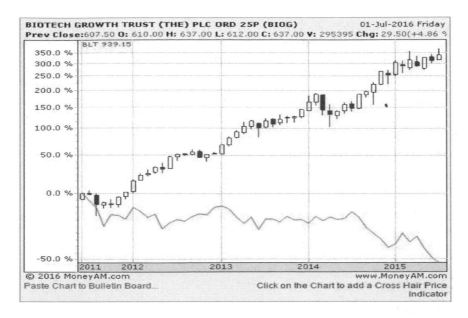

Figure 9. *Relative Strength Comparison between two stocks.*

An investor deciding whether to buy Biotech Growth Trust (black and white line) or BHP Billiton (black narrow line) should select BIOG (black and white line). That's because Biotech Growth Trust exhibits higher relative strength. A useful analogy to explain relative strength is to think back to your school days, and decide which student you would select if you had the opportunity to share in their future earnings. Would it be the person who had excelled at everything, or the person who flunked everything? It is far better to select the person that excelled (although there are occasional exceptions). The same logic applies to trading. Furthermore, bull markets only have a limited lifespan, so we are looking to maximise gains during the periods when the market is prime for trend-following strategies, it is no use investing in slouchy stocks.

Relative strength is an easy to use, and highly effective, indicator. Whether you are seeking to identify the best individual stocks or deciding which market to trade, assessing relative strength will help to identify the trade most likely to offer high returns.

Investing using relative strength works well with trend-following techniques. This is because when trend-following we are not necessarily making investments in assets that we believe have a great future. Instead we are buying because the market has indicated that other investors believe that these assets are highly desirable and have outstanding prospects.

Stock market history shows that traders who go with the flow of the market outperform those who fight against it. Provided stop losses are utilised correctly then trading strategies which rely on relative strength as a key indicator can be comparatively low risk compared to traditional buy and hold strategies.

10. Identifying Trades

Using a stock selection criterion helps identify outstanding stocks, otherwise a great stock could be seen, but its outstanding profit potential could be unrecognised. The two primary technical indicators used to identify outstanding stocks are high relative strength and a strong price trend.

The optimal time to enter a trend is when the price breaks out from a narrow trading range. These trades offer the best risk / reward ratio because the move higher is likely to be substantial, but if the trade fails it is only a short distance before the stop loss (which is located just below the low point of the narrow trading range) is hit, meaning that trades with this setup offer the potential for minimal losses but large gains. Therefore, we are searching for stock charts which form narrow trading ranges and rise strongly when they breakout, signalling that these stocks have high relative strength. Such stocks are not overly common, but we are seeking elite stocks exhibiting characteristics that signal outperformance and therefore their occurrence should not be expected to be abundant. However, within the leading sector of the market these characteristics will be much more prevalent. Therefore, traders should focus on identifying the leading sector and the best performing stocks within this sector. This provides a shortcut to identifying the best trading opportunities.

The chart of Darty Plc on the following page shows an example of a stock with high relative strength forming narrow trading ranges providing low risk / high reward trading opportunities.

Figure 10. *Darty Plc - A High Relative Strength Stock Forming Narrow Trading Ranges.*

In later chapters we will examine several trades where relative strength provided a potent indicator, and stocks were aggressively bought when breaking out from narrow trading ranges. These examples demonstrate the importance of relative strength for successful trading.

In my own trading, relative strength combined with trend-following are vital indicators. Relative strength is one of the most widely used and highly regarded indicators by many of the world's elite traders.

The simplicity of using the relative strength indicator combined with its accuracy in identifying outstanding stocks make it one of the best indicators available for trading any market.

10.1 Why Use Trend-Following

The simplicity and accuracy of trend-following strategies makes them the most potent tool in the technical analysis tool box. There is no other technical analysis methodology which has given such outstanding results to its disciples. People like John Henry, owner of Liverpool Football Club and the Boston Red Socks has accumulated over $1bn following trends. There are large numbers of successful trend-following traders providing irrefutable evidence that trend-following works.

Bull markets are long periods of optimism when prices trend higher. They typically last over 3 years, making them ideal to trade using trend-following strategies. Bear markets are shorter, but trend-following often gives excellent signals to capture gains from these movements. Markets often undergo large changes in valuation, leaving traders who are reliant on methods of fundamental valuation flummoxed and unable to participate in the market. Sometimes markets become very expensive, other times they become depressed and cheap. This suggests that markets are not an efficient mechanism for pricing assets. Therefore, making trading decisions based on the fundamental value of a company alone is often unwise. This is well illustrated by looking at the history of the stock market. The 1970's were pessimistic times with stocks trading on very low valuations, often as low 10 times earnings. But the 1980's saw investor optimism rise, and by the year 2000 stock markets were trading at over 25 times earnings. Trend-following traders could operate in any of these markets with equanimity.

The underlying reason why markets are prone to large swings is that the market's price is derived from the amalgamation of investor's assessment about the market. But investors make imperfect judgments, often causing the market to be grossly mispriced. Sometimes investors worry that the future will be very bleak, but at other times they become wildly optimistic, resulting in the formation of trends as the market moves to reflect the change in opinion. The most extreme of market action occurs when markets enter cycles of boom and bust which result in large valuation changes and substantial trends that are ideally suited to trend-following strategies. These cycles are highly significant and will be discussed in detail later in the book.

10.2 Other Reasons to Trade Trends

Trend-following enables traders to operate with greater confidence during periods when the market is overvalued because trend-following is independent of valuation. Trend followers only exit trades when the trend reverses, not when valuations reach levels the trader considers excessive. Trend-following also provides an excellent methodology for trading commodities and foreign exchange. In these markets the fundamental value of the item traded is more difficult to assess, so traders need to be acutely aware of the market's trend to trade successfully. For example, there is no definitive method to assess how many dollars a barrel of oil is worth, or how many euros a dollar is worth. Trend-following skills equip a trader for any market. The renowned physicist Sir Isaac Newton, who frequently traded financial markets, realised that trading based on valuation alone was dangerous. During a market boom he is noted as saying 'I can calculate the motion of the heavenly bodies, but not the madness of people.'

The fact that predicting market movements based on reasoning derived from mathematical calculations of value is of limited use when trading was also not missed by the famous economist John Maynard Keynes. As well as being a respected economist he was also a highly competent trader. He realised that his own opinion about the market was often incorrect and that it was necessary to take the opinions of other market participants into account. He described the thinking speculators must undertake using an analogy based on a fictional competition, in which entrants are asked to choose from a set of six photographs of women to decide which is the most beautiful. Those who picked the face that most people had selected won. He said that a naive strategy is to choose the face that, in your own opinion, is the most beautiful. A more sophisticated contestant would focus on identifying the face that was most likely to be selected by the other judges. The beauty of trend analysis is that it provides information about the opinion of other people, and since they dictate where the market goes the information is invaluable.

The use of trends and price has other important advantages. It enables traders to assess a trade in terms of risk and reward because when price is used as the primary indicator a stop loss is set at a defined price level, restricting losses. A target price is also set where the trade will be profitably exited. Using this methodology, the risk and reward of each trade can be estimated, enabling the merits of each trade to be assessed. The risk is equal to the number of points distance to where the stop loss is located (which is at prior support) and the reward is the distance to the target price where the trade will be closed. This level must be at least 3 times the distance to support, because profitable trading requires a large margin of safety, so a minimum risk / reward ratio of 3:1 is necessary. The concept of risk and reward is the keystone for successful trading. Because it is so important we will later look at many practical examples of how to use this principle.

10.3 Identifying Powerful Trends

At any one time there are normally many markets with prices that are trending. Some trends are more suitable for trading than others, giving larger returns in a shorter time span. When trading trends, the first step is to identify powerful trends since they will provide the best returns. A variety of additional indicators help us to achieve this, each of which is now going to be discussed.

10.4 Stock Indexes

Stock indexes are important indicators. They represent the average value of a group of stocks. For example, the price of the FTSE 100 is the average value of the 100 largest companies in the UK. The Dow Jones is the average value of 30 large companies in the United States, and the S&P 500 is the average value of the 500 largest companies in the United States. For traders these indexes are potent indicators. They show the general direction that stocks are moving. This is important because rising markets attract buying interest, and are therefore likely to continue rising. In bull markets 80% of stocks rise. In bear markets a similar proportion of stocks fall. Therefore, in a bull market success is much more likely to be achieved if we are buying stocks. In a bear market the chances of making money buying stocks is slim, so short sales should be used to profit from falling prices. Indexes are important because they enable the determination of whether it is a bull market or a bear market, informing the trader of whether to be a buyer or seller of stocks.

Stock indexes are useful to traders in another way. They provide important confirmatory evidence when trading. If the stock index forms a large trading range lasting many months and then breaks out it is a good time to buy shares. That's because markets reflect the herd mentality of traders. When the market is in a trading range many traders won't buy or sell, they will watch the market, waiting to see which way the market moves. Once the market breaks out traders will then enter the market, propelling it further in the direction in which it broke out.

Stock indexes enable traders to identify which way the 'herd' is moving, enhancing the probability of profitable trades being made. It is always a good first step to identify which way the stock index is trending, then identify the leading sector of the market, and then identify the best stock within that sector. Trades should preferably be timed when the stock index breaks out from a multi month trading range, as this often signals a substantial movement of the market will occur in the direction of the breakout. If the stock that is being traded has a high relative strength then it should move by a much larger amount than the overall market, providing the trader with a higher return.

10.5 Interpreting Volume Patterns

In mathematics, volume refers to the amount of space occupied by an object, but in stock market terminology it refers to the number of shares traded. Volume provides an insightful gauge of market strength, providing data about how many trades were made on a particular market movement. The greater the trading activity, the greater the momentum of the move and the greater the probability of the market continuing in that direction. High volume is of particular interest when occurring as the price breaks out from a trading range, or when the price gaps. Additionally, volume of more than twice the daily average is significant if it accompanies a price rise more of more than 5%. Over this threshold, the greater the volume and the greater the size of the price move the better the signal that the price will continue to move in that direction. The senses of the astute trader are quickened when volumes of five or even ten times the average daily volume occur and are accompanied by large price increases. High trading volume provides definitive confirmation that the stock has attracted significant investor attention. How the price performs during these times is particularly informative.

On very high volume days when the market is moving upwards it is important to see the stock close the trading session in the top half of the day's trading range, and even better to see it finish in the top

10% as this indicates that any selling pressure was absorbed with relative ease and that the end result of heavy trading was that the higher prices were sustained with ease. In contrast to this, a highly negative trading signal is given if a stock charges higher, rising over 5% on heavy trading volume but is unable to sustain the move and ends the day lower. This shows that the buying interest soon became overwhelmed by selling pressure, signalling the market is weak and that caution is warranted.

10.6 Using Moving Averages

A moving average is the average price of a stock over a period of time. For example, the 200 day moving average is the average price of the stock over the past 200 trading days. Using moving averages helps traders discern the trend more easily, since it removes the noise from the daily price moves. The most potent moving average for long term trend-following is the 200 day moving average, although there are several successful trend-following systems that use shorter term moving averages such as the 20 day and 50 day. Traders of medium to long term trends should buy when the 200 day moving average is sloping upwards and sell when the 200 day moving average is sloping downwards.

10.7 Using 52 Week Highs

The stock market consists of many thousands of stocks, so identifying the very best stocks could be time consuming. Fortunately, a simple method exists that will help identify every great stock. That's because great stocks all provide a single unmistakable signal before skyrocketing in value; they first reach a 52 week high in price. Using the list of stocks hitting new 52 week highs is like having a radar identifying every great stock.

Because the list of stocks hitting new 52 week highs is recognised by experienced traders as a great tool many financial websites allow users to view the list free of charge, although others impose a small charge. I use this list as my primary filter for identifying trading opportunities when the market is trending higher. The names of the best companies frequent the list with greatest repetition as they continually reach new 52 week highs, as if to remind traders that they are worthy of re-examination. Looking at the list also provides a valuable insight as to which sectors of the market are leaders and have the best relative strength.

The counterparty to the 52 week high list is the 52 week low list. In a bear market the weakest stocks that are leading the market lower need to be identified. The list of 52 week lows detects these stocks, identifying them as prime candidates for short selling.

10.8 All-time Highs in Price

Stocks that reach all-time highs are of particular interest because all-time high prices signal especially strong buying interest. The supply / demand situation in markets hitting all-time highs is particularly favourable for the market continuing to rise. Stocks at all-time highs encounter less selling pressure, and are therefore more likely to rise quickly. To explain; investors who supply stocks into a market (the sellers) can be grouped into three categories. Firstly, there are traders who are seeking to exit the market at a break-even level. They have previously bought stock and are looking to recover losses and sell when the price reaches break-even. The second category of sellers are those who bought at a lower price and hold a profitable position. Many of these holders will sell if the stock reaches the previous all-time high in price, or a price close to that level. Finally, there are short sellers who have borrowed stock and sold it with the hope that it will fall in value. They intend to buy it back at a lower price, hence making a profit. When a stock price rises to near its prior all time high many traders sell short the stock, betting that when it reaches the zone near the all-time high, the rally will fail and the price will fall. These three categories of seller are absent once the stock exceeds its all-time high because they have already sold. Much of the stock that they sold has passed into the hands of new holders, many of whom are long term holders. Facing lower selling pressure, the stock price can now advance rapidly. Moreover, on exceeding the all-time high, every bet placed by short sellers that the move higher would fail is losing money, so short sellers become anxious to close their trades. To do this they must buy back the stock they sold, creating additional buying pressure which moves the price even higher. Stocks reaching new all-time highs have an increased chance of rising since they face lower selling pressure.

Buying shares in Apple or Microsoft when their name first appeared on the list of new all-time highs proved a great time to buy, with the price subsequently zooming up several thousand percent. All stocks which are stellar performers first achieve new all-time highs in price, and their names then frequently re-appear on the list as they motor higher, making the list of stocks hitting new all-time highs an excellent radar for identifying outstanding stocks.

The counterpart to the all-time high list is the all-time low list. In a bear market the weakest stocks that are leading the market lower need to be identified. The list of all-time lows identifies these stocks.

10.9 Gaps

The intention of the successful trader is to accurately assess the market's strength, making gaps an extremely important technical indicator. Gaps occur when the price leaps, skipping from one price to another without trading, leaving a price gap where the stock didn't trade. When a share price gaps higher on positive news it is an excellent indicator that the news was materially better than the market expected, causing the price to leap. Trading signals from gap price moves have amplified significance when the gap results in the stock price breaking out from a trading range.

In an up-trending market gaps exhibit their most tradable signals when the price gaps away from a range where the market has traded for at least 6 weeks. Yet more significance is added if the price increase takes a stock to new 52 week, or all-time high. Further importance should be conferred to gaps which occur on trading days when the share price moves by a large amount as this indicates that the news was materially different to what the market expected. Because markets are rarely able to fully price in a major change in the fortunes of a stock in just one trading session the possibility of a sustained price change in future trading sessions is increased. Gaps that occur in the direction of the long term market trend are much more likely to signal the start of a sustainable move in that direction than those that are counter trend.

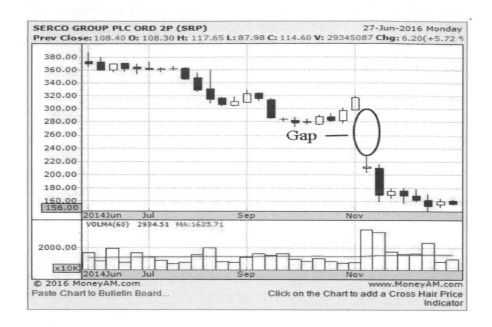

Figure 11. *Serco Plc Gaps Lower on Heavy Trading Volume.*

The chart of Serco Plc shows a price gap in a downtrend. The price gaps lower from 313p to 237p on triple the average daily trading volume, providing a strong indication of weakness and an excellent indicator that the downtrend will continue.

Gaps are an extremely potent indictor because their presence informs that the market has experienced an event that was not previously foreseen. For this reason the presence of gaps often portends to information that can cause a sustainable revaluation of the share price. Gaps, particularly when they occur as the share price breaks out from a trading range are of special importance because they often represent outstanding trading opportunities. We will look at several examples of this later on.

On certain occasions gaps are not indicative that the trend will continue, and may in fact be about to reverse. If a gap or series of gaps occur following a very large and rapid price change then the gap(s) can signal that the move is nearly exhausted and a reversal is imminent. Typically, these gaps (known as exhaustion gaps) occur after a run up in price of 50% or more in less than 5 months. Note: gaps on FOREX charts, commodities and stock indexes should generally be ignored as they normally occur due to technical factors associated being traded on various different global markets.

10.10 Summary

The indicators discussed in this chapter provide traders with the tools necessary to identify excellent trading opportunities. Each indicator, when used in isolation, improves the probability of trading success. The probability of achieving exceptional results improves as the number of reliable indicators signalling that the price is going to make a substantial move increases.

The use of low quality indicators is a common cause for poor trading. Quality is far more important than quantity. It is important to only use the indicators that have the highest reliability, which is why in this book only indicators that are proven to enhance trading performance are discussed.

11. Chart Analysis

We've talked the talk, now it's time to walk the walk

Having identified our preferred trading indicators and understanding the information they convey it is necessary to test our abilities.

In this chapter we examine a series of charts and seek to identify the opportunities that have the most favourable risk reward ratio and hence present the best trading opportunities. The opportunities we will examine are those when the price exhibits the characteristics of gaps, relative strength and breakouts from trading ranges, with a focus on identifying narrow trading ranges and the outstanding trading opportunities that are often associated with this trading signal.

We will examine charts which are in uptrends and downtrends and therefore we will be seeking to identify opportunities to buy when the price is in an uptrend and offers trading opportunities to profit from rising prices. When the price is trending lower the focus will be on identifying opportunities to sell short.

Q. Examine the chart of Ryanair Holdings on the following page. Can you identify the trading range breakout with a gap and high trading volume?

A: The breakout occurs in the first week of November 2014. The price gaps out of a trading range on heavy volume, exceeding 800p. The catalyst for the breakout was an announcement of company earnings exceeding market expectations, triggering a new uptrend as the share price rose to reflect faster than expected earnings growth.

It is common for a single piece of good news to be the catalyst for a stock to undertake a significant rally. Often the price will rise in excess of 20% as a result of earnings beating expectations. In this instance we know that the news was better than the market anticipated because trading volume increased to more than double the average on the day that the news was released and the price gapped higher. This informs the observant trader that the probability of further increases in the value of the stock was high since the surge in volume and price suggests that investors were desperate to buy the stock because prospects are materially better than was previously thought. This buying interest often persists, causing a rally in the stock price that can last many months. Traders who buy stocks shortly after positive announcements that triggers large increases in trading volume and price gaps often capture significant profits as the stock price re-rates to incorporate the improving prospects for the company.

2. Identify the low risk trade entry points onto Skyepharma's trend.

A: The best trading opportunity occurs when the share price breaks out from the narrow trading range which forms between 115p -120p. Note how the share price breaks out from this trading range on high volume signalling a significant new move higher. Other good trading opportunities also occur. Between 80p and 85p the price forms a narrow trading range and then breaks out on high volume. The price then returns towards the breakout level, providing another opportunity to buy. In this instance the stop loss should be set just below the lows of the trading range from which the breakout occurred i.e. at 78p.

A further narrow trading range forms between 180p and 200p from which the price also breaks out on high volume. This also presents another good trading opportunity.

Q. Examine the chart of McBride . Identify the low risk entry points onto the uptrend in McBride stock.

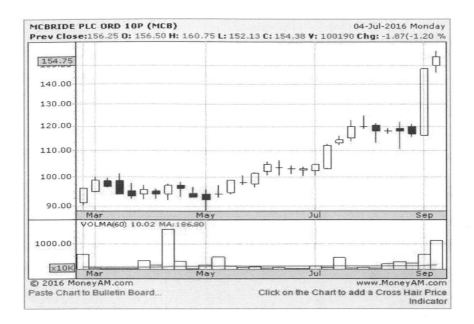

A: The first low risk buy signal occurs when the price breaks above £1.00 in June, with a stop loss positioned just below the low point prior to the break out (at 96p). McBride's stock price then forms a tight trading range between 100 and 105p. The price breaks out above 105p giving another excellent low risk opportunity to buy. The stop loss for this trade is set at the lows of the trading range that the stock has just broken out from, at 100p. Yet another opportunity occurs in mid-September when the price breaks out from a narrow trading range above 120p. The stop loss can be set at the most recent lows of the prior trading range, at 117p.

It is worth noting when looking at McBride's chart how the price ascent is slow at first, but momentum builds as the evidence that the company has brightening prospects becomes increasingly apparent. It is relatively common for a stock's price to remain range bound for prolonged periods at the beginning of a new trend and then for momentum to build as the stock begins its ascent. For this reason traders should not be overly disheartened if a stock performs sluggishly when it breaks out from a large trading range at the beginning of a new uptrend because it takes time for more evidence to emerge about the stocks' improving prospects and for other traders to become aware of the company's improving situation.

It is also worth pointing out that the price of this stock increased strongly despite the rest of the market trading in a sideways range, signalling increasing relative strength. It is when multiple factors such as a breakout from a trading range occurs, accompanied by other factors such as high volume, a price gap, and improving relative strength that trades are likely to earn large returns. The greater the number of positive indicators that signal to buy the greater the likelihood of earning a large return.

It is never advisable to trade based on only one indicator. Successful traders seek out multiple high quality indicators that support the case for making the trade

Q. Examine the chart of Blur Group Plc. Can you identify the best the entry point?

A. The prime opportunity to enter the uptrend arises on the breakout from the first narrow trading range at 170p, with the stop loss being positioned at the low point of the trading range from which the breakout occurred.

Other opportunities arise later in the trend when the price forms a narrow trading range and then breaks out above 500p in December 2013. These opportunities are less attractive owing to the trading ranges from which the stock broke out from being wider with support and resistance also less well defined.

Blur's chart shows the uptrend fail when support at 420p fails on high trading volume, giving a powerful sell signal.

12. Trading Trends

"Change always brings opportunities" – Nido Qubein

In 2003 the charts indicated that the market's major downtrend had ended, and that the market was pregnant with a major new bull market. I needed to identify stocks that would trend powerfully higher in the embryonic bull market and the technology sector was an obvious place to look. Advances in information technology were continually producing new companies that went on to outperform. However, my understanding of technology was limited, and I was concerned about the rapid rate of obsolescence that dogged the sector. I remember an old trader telling me that all technology companies were toaster companies. Having seen many instances of cutting edge technology become mundane in only a few years I knew he was making an important point about the rate of obsolescence. Instead of investing in technology stocks I searched for growth stocks with exposure to emerging markets, since the opportunities in these markets were bright.

The past 10 years had seen strong growth in emerging markets. It seemed logical that the improved communication offered by the growth of the internet would mean doing business in emerging markets would become simpler and quicker, giving increased cost advantages to emerging economies. A small company called International Trade Exhibitions (ITE) was identified as having good prospects. They organised trade exhibitions in emerging markets. It was well-established, holding market leading positions in many sectors. The bear market that had started in 2001 had caused the stock's price to slide from 120p to a low price of just 11p (see fig 12.

below). The stock price had since partially recovered and had just broken out, trading at 42p. In the forthcoming year the company wasn't expected to be profitable as subpar economic growth in emerging markets dented attendance levels at key exhibitions.

I was confident emerging market growth would recover. Emerging markets had less debt, more dynamism and expanding populations, indicating superior long term prospects.

Despite the strong long term factors that favoured emerging markets analysts were pessimistic, with no growth in earnings forecast for the current year or the following year, meaning the stock failed to meet Slater's requirements to invest. However, the stock was in an uptrend and technical analysis indicated an excellent trading opportunity.

Technical analysis said the stock was a buy, but Slater's system didn't; it was a dilemma - how should this situation be traded? The next section is about making that decision.

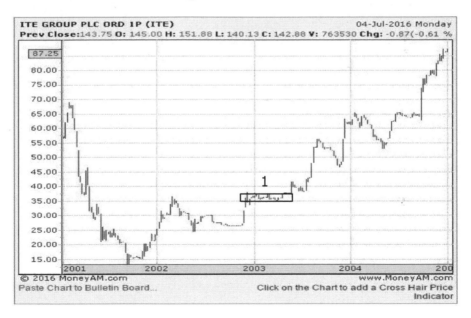

Figure 12. *Chart of ITE Plc.*

Figure 12 (above) shows ITE share price transitioning from a downtrend in 2001 into a new uptrend. A narrow trading range began forming in December 2002 (marked 1), lasting 5 months. This period of stability signalled support for the share price.

It had risen strongly in the previous 15 months, yet sufficient buying occurred to maintain the share price at a price near to its recent high, indicating buyers thought the shares good value. Another reason for liking ITE was that it was a high relative strength stock, since bottoming at 11p 15 months ago it had increased over 300%, whereas most stocks had risen less than 50%.

The other critical rationale for buying was that the move higher in ITE was confirmed by the movements of many other vitally important stock indexes such as the German stock market (DAX 30) and S&P 500 index in the United States. They gave buy signals as they broke out from major downtrends and established new powerful uptrends. In the U.K the FTSE 100 stock index had also established a new uptrend. For the FTSE 100, this occurred when it traded above key resistance at 4200 (see Fig 13 on next page), signalling a new bull market.

The price of the FTSE 100 represents the value of the 100 largest companies in the UK. When it moved above 4200 it signalled the downtrend had reversed for most stocks in the UK heralding a new bull market. This was the confirmation signal to buy.

ITE performed superbly, but the majority of the shares were quickly sold because, although ITE did very well, the performance of certain other stocks was unexpectedly superior. Oil exploration stocks and mining stocks became the runaway leaders of the new bull market. Knowing that relative strength was an excellent indicator of continued outperformance I decided to switch a significant portion of my investment into oil and mining stocks anticipating that this diversification would reduce risk and improve performance. I did this even though the market hadn't ever shown much interest in these sectors because commodity prices had been depressed for a very long time, so I hadn't any experience investing in the mining or oil sector.

Figure 13. *Chart of FTSE 100.*

There were many ways to profit from the rise in commodity prices other than buying shares in mining and oil companies. Commodities could be bought, for example gold or oil, using cash or on margin from a broker. Alternatively, the currencies of commodity producing nations were rising as their economies boomed on the back of windfall profits from rising commodity prices, offering profit opportunities by trading currencies.

I decided to focus exclusively on investing in the stocks of mining and oil companies. This was because stocks multiplied the gains which were occurring in the underlying commodity. For example, an oil company produces oil for $30 per barrel and the current market price is $40 per barrel then the company makes a profit of $10 per barrel. If the price rises to $50 per barrel, then profits double to $20 per barrel. In comparison if oil was bought at $40 per barrel and the price rose to $50 per barrel only 25% profit would be attained.

Selection of the correct asset class proved essential to maximising profits from the huge price increases in commodities. Profits at mining companies multiplied as the value of the underlying commodities they produced increased.

12.3 Five Great Stocks

A primary assertion of this book is that great stocks have common characteristics. A trader who knows these characteristics and is able to identify them will enjoy higher success rates than those unable to read the market's signals. Economic cycles and product cycles are long term and therefore such cycles tend to create trends that last for many years. Trend-following enables the early recognition of these trends and enables traders to maximise their return from the occurrence of major trends.

In this section we look at five stocks which performed outstandingly well to illustrate the common characteristics of great stocks and how to identify them using technical analysis and news flow analysis, and also to show that to earn large profits in the stock market investors do not have to take large risks.

When examining the charts of these stocks the high relative strength of each stock should be noted. Between 2003 and 2007 stock indexes such as the FTSE 100, DAX and Dow Jones increased by approximately 50%. All of the stocks featured in this chapter increased many times more than the market. They signalled their strength early in the bull market and continued to outperform for many years, rewarding investors who identified the early signs of strength with large returns.

Not only did these stocks emit technical signals that they were strong, they also grew earning per share rapidly. Examination of the fundamentals told investors that they were enjoying booming demand. Because these stocks were growing profits rapidly the market struggled to re-rate the share price quickly enough, meaning they traded on low valuations relative to their growth rate (i.e. they had a low PEG ratio)

Charter Plc

Charter Plc's business was linked to the boom in commodities and the associated construction boom in China that was driving up the price of many commodities. It specialised in supplying equipment for welding and cutting metals.

Economic growth in China and other emerging markets required the construction of large infrastructure projects and this construction necessitated the use of the type of equipment that Charter Plc manufactured, causing the company's profits to multiply as demand soared. During the boom the company often traded on a lowly forward PE ratio of less than 15, which was the approximate average valuation for all stocks at this time, yet the stock massively outperformed the overall market.

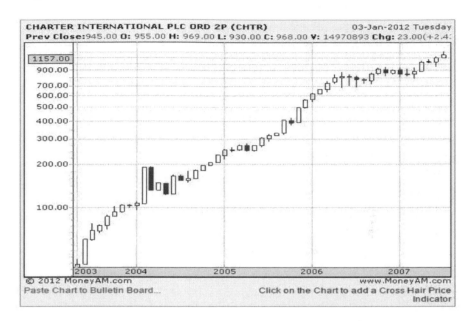

Figure 14. *Charter International Plc.*

From a trading perspective Charter Plc was a particularly attractive stock because it frequently traded in very narrow trading ranges. When the stock broke out from these trading ranges it provided low risk opportunities to add to positions. Also, because the trend was well defined, identifying a change in the direction of the trend, should it have occurred, would have been simple.

Aquarius Platinum

The boom in commodities triggered the price of mining stocks to rise powerfully, with most starting to run higher by 2003. However, platinum mining stocks didn't begin their move higher until they broke out in 2005.

Expanding mine production and surging platinum prices meant analysts' estimates for earnings were constantly ratcheted higher, providing the fuel behind the share price rise.

Aquarius Platinum had an established production base meaning it wasn't dependent upon making new discoveries for its future profits. This helped make investment in the company a low risk investment to benefit from the global bull market in commodities that was driving huge increases in the share prices of mining companies. Tighter worldwide emissions standards meant soaring platinum demand for catalytic converters, especially from countries such as China which were experiencing rapid growth in car usage and growing pollution problems.

Figure 15. *Aquarius Platinum Plc.*

Aquarius Platinum exhibited outstanding relative strength immediately following its breakout above 100p. The stock then formed numerous trading ranges presenting opportunities to enter low risk trades. Within 3 years of breaking out from the trading range it had formed below 100p the stock had risen 900%.

When investing in stocks that are in the leading sector of a bull market such gains are not unusual. The important task for all traders is to identify when a new trend has occurred. Typically this is following a recession or other period of market turbulence that has resulted in a significant market decline.

The other aspects to investing, other than finding great investments, is holding them whilst substantial profits accrue. Fear of losing profits causes traders to abandon trends prematurely. Using a suitable trend-following system is vital to being able to hold onto quality investments.

In the eventuality that market volatility does cause a trend to be exited prematurely good trading skills will facilitate re-joining the trend with minimal risk.

Tullow Oil Plc

Tullow Oil's business is oil exploration and production. It had a stable portfolio of oil producing assets, but the company was also exploring some highly prospective areas of Africa. The profits from the company's portfolio of oil producing assets helped lessen the volatility caused by the successes and failures of its exploration program, making its trend more stable than those oil companies which were totally reliant on exploration success. This helped make the stock highly suitable for trend-following and an excellent stock for medium to longer term trend-followers. Company earnings were constantly upgraded from 2003-2007 as rising oil prices and exploration success multiplied profits. Tullow Oil shows that achieving exceptionally high returns needn't entail huge risks and that a sweet spot exists where the optimal risk / reward ratio occurs. Rarely is the optimal risk reward ratio found in stocks which have no profits and no established track record of success. These types of stocks occasionally do offer large returns but the risk of owning them is routinely underestimated by investors

Owing to the importance of investing in stocks which are likely to be in the 'sweet spot' between risk and return several case studies later in the book will provide the reader with guidance on identifying stocks that are optimally positioned and highlight some of the dangers associated with investing in stocks without an established earning stream. With any successful stock it is often the case that success begets more success.

Figure 16. *Tullow Oil Plc.*

Tullow's success with the drill bit caused takeover stories to swirl, pushing the price of the stock even higher.

Many newcomers to investing are drawn to highly speculative stocks in the belief that this is the only way to earn large returns. Evidence shows that it is not necessary to invest in stocks engaged in high risk endeavours to earn large returns.

Fenner Plc

Fenner Plc is another example of a stock that wasn't directly exposed to the daily or weekly volatility of booming commodity prices. As long as commodity prices remained high enough for new exploration to be viable Fenner's business would grow since it manufactured items for the exploration and production of minerals and oil. This meant the stock was high growth / low volatility, ideal for trend-following

Fenner's share price soon established a strong uptrend that offered traders using trend-following techniques the opportunity of large profits.

Figure 17. *Fenner Plc.*

Fenner regularly updated the market on its progress, often advising that results would exceed market expectations. The commentary about trading and the outlook given in the company's financial report were optimistic which provided excellent guidance for traders and investors. For example, on the 8th November 2006 the company announced profits were up 136 percent and gave a confident statement about the outlook for the company. The dividend was also increased.

Fenner is yet another example which illustrates that high risk investments are not necessary to achieve high rewards. Fenner's share price gain wasn't as a result of a new product or a risky venture, it was simply the result of exposure to a sector that was experiencing booming demand. Provided the trader invests in the sector with the highest relative strength, but doesn't invest in stocks which are overly dependent on outcomes which will make the stock's price highly volatile, buying stocks which are low risk but give high returns is possible provided a system of trend-following is used to enable the trend to be exited once it expires.

In later chapters we look at boom bust cycles as this simplifies identifying the optimal time to invest in stocks that are about to experience explosive growth.

ITE Plc

ITE was exposed to the booming economic growth in emerging markets and also the commodities boom since many of the company's largest exhibitions were for the oil and gas industry and took place in emerging markets. Rising oil and gas prices meant strong economic growth in countries such as Russia which produced large volumes of hydrocarbons. ITE held many of its key exhibitions in emerging markets that also produced hydrocarbons, causing strong growth in earnings as companies in the sector increased their marketing budgets.

Figure 18. *ITE Plc.*

The trend in ITE stock formed a narrow trading range which enabled low risk entry onto the trend. By the end of the bull market in emerging markets and commodities ITE's stock price was trading at £3.20, driven by surging earnings growth. This amounted to a gain in the share price of over 800% from the beginning of the bull market to its end.

12.4 Lessons Learned

Firstly, charts provide crucial information about the market's trend. The direction of the trend is the most important indicator for traders, defining whether to be a buyer or seller. Some trends are more suitable for trading than others. Stocks which rise strongly and have low volatility are ideally suited to trend-following.

Secondly, following a recession the markets typically establish a new uptrend before company earnings improve. If a trader waits until company earnings increase before investing then a significant portion of the new uptrend will often be forfeited.

Thirdly, it is crucial that traders have regard to the trend direction of the major indexes such as the FTSE 100, DAX, NASDAQ and S&P 500 as these provide an overview of the market. If these indexes and the 200 day moving average are trending higher, and the share price is above the 200 day moving average line, then the trader should buy stocks. If any of these criteria are unfulfilled then the trade becomes less favourable.

Fourthly, during the early stages of an economic recovery it is very important to identify the best performing sector, as it is likely to continue outperforming. Many web sites publish tables showing how each sector has performed over the past 1 month, 3 months, 6 months and 1 year. In the early stages of an economic recovery the primary aim of a trader is to identify low risk opportunities to invest in quality stocks in the leading sector.

Fifthly, traders often have a wide variety of methods to benefit from a new trend. For example, the trend higher in commodities could have been exploited by buying a commodity, for example oil.

Alternatively, buying stocks in a country that will prosper because of high oil prices, or buying the currency of a commodity producing country. Whatever developments occur, careful consideration should be made of what asset class to buy, as this can make a huge difference in the amount of profit earned from an investment idea.

Sixth, as well as investing in the stocks of the leading sector, exposure can be supplemented by investing in an Exchange Traded Fund (ETF). ETF's invest in a large number of stocks that are specific to a sector of the market and are available for almost every market sector. Sector specific ETF's, such as the Basic Resources ETF, or the Biotech ETF, are now available to trade on most trading platforms. They diversify risk across the sector, removing company specific risk. ETFs often have much lower volatility than individual stocks, making them more suitable for trend-following strategies than investing in the individual companies that comprise the ETF.

Finally, during the Californian gold rush of the 1850's several miners stuck it rich, but most miners were not so fortunate, and lost money. Independently of the fortunes of the individuals who actually mined the gold, the merchants who sold the miners their picks, shovels and other provisions normally made much more money and enjoyed a more consistent earnings stream than those miners who risked their lives.

The lesson is that during booms, whichever sector they occur in, there are often lower risk businesses offering superior returns. The share price movements of these companies are often suited to trend-following strategies because they offer investors a more visible stream of earnings, resulting in the stock price having a smoother price trend. Charter, Fenner and ITE are examples of companies that profited greatly from improving conditions in the markets that they operated in, yet they were not involved in high risk activities. These companies are the modern day equivalent of the merchants who sold the picks and axes to the miners during the Californian gold rush. They were optimally positioned on the risk / reward spectrum to profit from the boom provided traders used trend-following strategies when making the investment, so that once the boom subsided they exited the trades, hence avoiding the substantial downside risks that arise when economic booms expire. Without the use of trend-following such trades would be too risky to undertake.

13. Darvas' System

Trend-following transformed the performance of my trading, enabling identification of the best stocks and signalling low risk entry points to trade and, although mistakes still happened, trading yielded good profits. For the first time, becoming a competent trader seemed achievable, but to ensure continued success I needed to learn more. Life was too short to learn how to trade via trial and error, continuing to study the observations and experiences of elite traders was crucial, but finding the best books wasn't easy, with many thousands of trading books available. I had learned to avoid academic style textbooks, as they were the least informative. From several hundred pages there might only be a few pages containing useful information, with the rest of the book filled with theoretical technical analysis that didn't work.

I noticed the best books weren't written by people with PhD's or specialist qualifications in market analysis, they were written by people who had succeeded in making money from the markets themselves. The format of my preferred book was simply: this is what I did, and this is how I did it. The book 'How I Made $2 Million Dollars In The Stock Market' was one such book; it really helped me learn how to trade.

The book was written by a world famous professional dancer, Nicolas Darvas, who made a $2,000,000 fortune trading markets as he toured the world with his dancing troupe and, when the public learned of his success it caused a sensation. The public were desperate to learn his winning techniques and he responded by publishing a book, which instantly became a bestseller.

In the book he revealed his trading methods in explicit detail. He had entered the stock market without any particular intention to do so when he was offered payment for his work, not in money, but in stock. He accepted and became a shareholder for the first time. The gain on his first investment was outstanding and the stock was sold for a substantial profit. He immediately sought similar stocks, but repeating his prior success proved difficult. Darvas thought professional advice would help him to achieve his goal so he began subscribing to stock market tip sheets and consulting stock brokers. Unfortunately the professional advice also disappointed. He could find no way to replicate the exceptional initial rate of return. In desperation he embarked on his own analysis of company financial reports, thinking that this would guide him. But after studying many reports he realised 'company reports can tell you the past and the present, but not the future'. He was frustrated, but not about to give up. Convinced a way existed for selecting the very best stocks, he persevered. After searching for several years he found the solution. It wasn't in company reports, stock market tip sheets, or the brains of stockbrokers. He found that the answer lay in the price of the stock itself, and the way it moved.

Darvas realised that great stocks were identifiable by their stronger than average price performance. Rather than trying to find stocks that he thought were great businesses, he focused on identifying stocks the market indicated it liked. He identified them by examining their price performance, looking for stocks that had a high relative strength. Darvas' eureka moment was when he realised 'the market tells its own story best'. He went on to devise a simple but ingenious method to stay invested in stocks that were rising, but which gave a timely sell signal when the market weakened.

His technique was to monitor the price movements and trading volume of stocks he thought were suitable candidates for trading and if, for example, he identified a stock in an uptrend with very high relative strength and the stock was trading in a range between $2.65 and $3.10 he would buy only if it broke above $3.10 and sell only if it couldn't maintain its price within the new trading range. Darvas' approach to the market had both a funnelling and filtering effect. Weak stocks were filtered out and his resources funnelled into stronger stocks. Furthermore, he used stop losses on all trades to limit downside risk. He allowed profits to grow until the price demonstrated signs of exhaustion, leaving his trades free to achieve unlimited upside. This resulted in his trading record having many highly profitable trades and many small losses. In his book he writes that the reason for his success was that 'I was successful in taking larger profits than losses in proportion to the amount invested'.

His technique meant that he was never fighting against the market's trend, and because his approach to trading weeded out stocks when they lagged his funds were quickly re-deployed, resulting in his portfolio undergoing a process of continuous improvement.

Darvas called his trading method 'the box trading method', on the basis that he would draw a box around the trading range that the stock was in and only buy when the price traded above the previous high points of that box. An example of the type of stock that he sought to identify is shown in below.

Figure 19. *Chart Showing Box Trading Method.*

1) Buy when the price rises above the prior highs of the box into a new range

2) Sell if the price falls into the previous box. The chart of Powerflute Plc (figure 19) shows boxes marked around the trading ranges, providing an example of how to use the box trading method. The price pattern resembles a series of boxes stacked one on top of the other. Stocks which trade in narrow trading ranges for a time frame of several weeks or months are especially suited to the box trading method. Multiple narrow trading ranges within an uptrend are an excellent indication that the stock has outstanding prospects. From a risk and reward perspective they also represent outstanding trading opportunities.

The first advantage of Darvas' methodology is that it is clearly discernible when the stock exceeds the top of its range, giving a buy signal. Secondly, a clear signal is given if the stock has weakened and should be exited (when the price penetrates a lower box). This type of chart pattern, when the stock trades in a narrow range for several weeks or months, is commonly referred to as a narrow trading range or flag, and is one of the very few types of highly reliable patterns. A study by Bulkowski, in his book The Encyclopaedia of Chart Patterns [2] concluded that:

'The average rise following a breakout above the top of the flag at 63%, is among the highest I have seen for any formation.' A frequency distribution suggests that the most likely rise is a more sedate 20% to 30%. However, 33% of the formations have gains over 90% and 44% have gains over 50% in about 2 months. A 50% gain in about 2 months is a formation worth exploring!'

My own trading experiences strongly concur with Bulkowski's findings. Many successful traders focus solely on trading this type of price formation. Darvas, without using rigorous scientific methods had discovered, many years before Bulkowski's study, that trading this type of pattern gives excellent results.

Darvas' system can also be used to profit from falling stock prices. Here's a challenge; can you identify how to trade HSS Hire Group Plc (below), identifying the best points to enter trades to profit from the falling price using Darvas' system?

Figure 20. *Chart of HSS Hire Group Plc.*

Answer: The first signal to short the stock occurs when the narrow trading range formed at between 185p and 210p fails and the price drops below 185p. In the last week of June the price gaps lower on heavy volume, signalling the trend to lower prices will continue. Another narrow trading range forms at 122p to 140p. When the low price of the 120-140p trading range fails the share price slumps again. A further box forms at the 60p price range and this also presents an opportunity to sell short. Short sales should be entered when the floor of each box is penetrated. This is shown in figure 21 on the following page.

Using the box trading methods helps simplify when trades should be executed because the boxes provide a clear line which when breached by the price triggers a trade to be opened. Also, using the box trading method clarifies how wide the trading range is, with the narrower trading ranges providing the best opportunities.

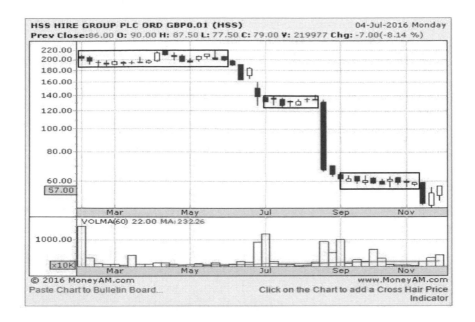

Fig 21. *Box Trading Method for Short Sales.*

Darvas' system proved highly successful, but he realised that no trading system is infallible. He confesses in his book 'I became over confident, and that is the most dangerous state of mind that anyone can develop in the stock market'. Even trading strategies which appear simple actually still require skill and emotional discipline.

The opportunities that Darvas traded are not common. Often there are only a few suitable stocks for this type of trade, so traders have to hunt for these opportunities.

Darvas hadn't developed his trading methodology without regard to the observations and experiences of previous generations of successful traders. I soon realised that he probably borrowed heavily from the ideas of a legendary trader called Richard Donchian, who published his trading ideas many years before Darvas. Donchian also used price signals to generate trading signals and understood the importance of trading systems being uncomplicated.

Donchian's methods have withstood the test of time. Traders who follow his methods will find a wide range of opportunities to trade because markets regularly give signals that indicate a trader should act. Donchian's trading systems remains widely used today in their purest form or they form the cornerstone of many strategies used by today's most successful traders. Many of today's strategies that seek to time trades by trading on the breakout from trading ranges are based on Donchian's methods.

The specifics of Donchian's trading system are given below.

Technique 1

When the price crosses above the 200 day moving average and closes that week's trading above the 200 day moving average, new buy trades should be opened, but only if the direction of the 200 day moving average is up.

Technique 2

Buy when the market price exceeds the highest high price of the last 4 weeks. Close the position when the price trades below the lowest low of the last 4 weeks or on a break below the 200 Day moving average.

Technique 3

Buy when the weekly closing price breaks out above the highest price of the last 12 weeks. Set the stop loss just below the lowest low of the past 4 weeks or on a break below the 200 day moving average.

If the breakouts are successful then stay invested as long as the current weekly close is above the 200 day moving average and the trend of the 200 day moving average is upwards.

Trades can be taken using any of these methods individually or in combination.

14. Decision Making

Decision making is an important part of trading, yet its importance is overlooked in many trading textbooks. However, decision making by the medical profession has been extensively studied and published, and one case study provided insights into decision making that were highly relevant to trading.

The case study detailed an instance where a hospital needed to improve its diagnosis rate for heart attacks. The hospital typically saw 30 patients per day who thought they had suffered a heart attack. The protocol for identifying heart attack victims was long, exhaustive, expensive, but very often inconclusive. The hospital's diagnosis procedure required answering a seemingly endless number of questions about symptoms and medical history. The hospital then used an ECG machine to gather more information. The principle behind diagnosis at this hospital was to gather as much information as possible and then make a decision. But the results were unacceptably inaccurate. Heart attack victims were being sent home without receiving the necessary treatment because of misdiagnosis. For improvement the hospital decided to employed mathematicians who specialised in the difficult task of categorising subatomic particles. The doctors hoped to use their expertise of categorisation to separate those who had suffered a heart attack from those who hadn't.

After analysing data about the risk factors for heart attacks the mathematicians decided that diagnosis should focus on data from the ECG machine and only three other factors, which would then be fed into an algorithm. The new method improved the number of correct diagnoses by 70%. The physicists had removed from the decision making process the data that the doctors thought was relevant, and focused on the data that was relevant.

So how could this help in making better judgements on the stock market? Having recently studied both Darvas' and Donchian's trading methods I realised that by focusing on the stocks' trend, trading volume and relative strength they had each created their own algorithm which excluded much of the data that was thought to be relevant, and focused on what was relevant. They had succeeded in eliminating the 'noise' that fogs an investor's decision making. The methodology developed by Jim Slater was successful for the same reason.

Lessons Learned

Firstly, it is important to critically analyse the reliability of trading indicators. If they haven't got the requisite reliability they are probably overcomplicating things, and negatively impacting decision making. Physicists often use the phrase 'hydrogen atom' as a metaphor for the simplest model that captures the essence of a situation, because the hydrogen atom is the simplest atom. There is strong evidence that trading systems which focus on capturing the essence of market behaviour earn superior returns.

Secondly, ideas and information to improve trading can be drawn from almost any subject area.

15. Things Go Wrong

Tanfield Plc – A company with rapid earnings growth, excellent products and no debt. It seemed perfect, what could go wrong?

The year was 2006 and the stock market had been trending higher since its lows three years ago. Because the market had risen substantially bargains were rare. I was scouting the market for new investment opportunities. I was cautious, the market had risen strongly and I didn't want to be complacent in investing new money at high prices.

The daily market scan of stocks hitting new 52 week price highs identified a company called Tanfield Plc which had that day broken out from a large trading range to reach a new 52 week high on heavy trading volume. The breakout foretold a powerful move higher was likely because the size of the price move when the stock broke out was multiples of the average daily move and the trading volume on the breakout was also multiples of the average. Checking the stock's P/E ratio and comparing it to the forecast growth rate signalled that the stock was cheap. In the current year the company was forecast to earn 1.22p rising to 3.40p in 2007 as the benefits of an aggressive growth strategy bore profits. With the stock trading just below 30p the explosive growth in earnings put the stock on a forward P/E ratio of below 8 times next year's earnings, which, for a stock forecast to grow earnings by over 200%, indicated outstanding value.

The company planned continued rapid growth in future years and, provided the economy remained strong, prospects were excellent.

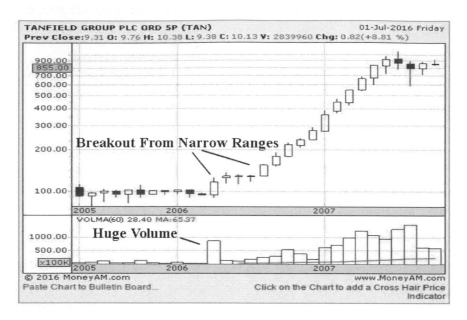

*Price on chart has been rebased because of stock split.

Fig 22. *(Above) Chart of Tanfield Plc breaking out heavy trading volume.*

Tanfield manufactured platforms for working at height which were used in the construction and maintenance of buildings. Demand was buoyant and there seemed no imminent reason for change. Another division of Tanfield manufactured specialist electric vehicles for use at airports, hospitals and parks. Demand was also strong, quadrupling in the past 2 years. A third division manufactured road going electric trucks with zero environmental emissions, meaning that vehicle surcharges to enter major cities such as London were avoided. Improvements in battery technology and high diesel prices were additional factors indicating that electric trucks were now a viable alternative to conventional diesel powered trucks. Growth was forecast to boom.

With technical analysis signalling to buy and superb growth forecasted Tanfield was exactly the type of stock that could give outstanding profits. I compulsively re-examined the chart of Tanfield, reviewing the company's annual reports and repeatedly compared its stock to other stocks that I held. The outcome was that I frequently sold other stocks to fund investment in Tanfield, until it became the largest trade on the account.

Good news from the company continued, rising oil prices meant that more and more companies trialled electric vehicles, seeking cost savings and a green image. The company announced plans to produce a small truck and collaborated with Ford on electric vehicles. The collaboration with Ford made Tanfield a world leader and sales soared.

Business at the aerial work platform business also boomed. A large acquisition had been made and production was being consolidated at a new factory which had recently been opened by the U.K Prime Minister. In only months the stock's value had doubled, and within 6 months it had tripled! This was the biggest single trade I had made and was already the most profitable. I spent many hours contemplating whether to sell some shares, but decided to allow the profits to run whilst the price was trending higher. However, on this occasion, the gains were unnervingly large, making the urge to take profits very strong.

I resisted selling and was rewarded by seeing earnings forecasts being ratcheted even higher and as the forecasts for profits grew so did the share price. My paper wealth was increasing faster than I ever dared to image. Some weeks the holdings value would increase by £10,000. Yet the happiness I expected to feel as many years of hard work and risk taking came to fruition was illusive. I expected that after spending years building a sufficient stake I would experience euphoria as the years of trading yielded results. Instead, I felt uneasy. I wanted to lock in some profits, yet on the balance of probabilities that wasn't the best action to take.

The stock market made another strong push higher. I became sure that Tanfield stock would soon succumb to profit taking and impulsively I sold 30% of my holding. After battling this desire for several months it only took only a moment to fail, I instantly recognised my mistake. Since purchase the stock had appreciated 300%, yet during this meteoric rise the price had never retreated more than 15%. Tanfield stock was unmoved by the temporary slide in the market. Its strength indicating that instead of selling I should have bought more. Having barely suffered during the market's wobble, Tanfield's stock price soon exploded higher. Several weeks later the company issued a trading update, saying that business momentum was strong; the stock surged even higher. Eight months from purchase and the stock had appreciated 700%. The impulsive act of selling proved expensive.

Then something unexpected happened. The share price tumbled for no apparent reason. The company was concerned about the way its stock price was falling and issued a statement reassuring shareholders, saying that it knew of no reason for the fall, and that trading was strong. But the fall in Tanfield's stock was not isolated; other construction and banking related stocks were suffering.

After the sharp sell-off Tanfield stock again experienced good buying interest. Its price rose along with other stocks in the market, causing traders to breathe a deep sigh of relief. However, the rally soon stalled and the stock price folded over, then crashed lower. It couldn't sustain even a small price increase without sellers flooding into the market and knocking the price back down again. Things had changed, the uptrend had failed and now the price was plunging lower through important support levels. Tanfield had been a low volatility stock in a stable uptrend, but it was now a highly volatile stock in a downtrend. Additionally, the way the share price moved changed, it was no longer stronger than the overall market. It had become weak and was now regularly one of the largest fallers in the market. When the market moved lower, Tanfield moved lower by a much greater amount than expected. This loss of strength signalled to sell the remaining shares I held. I had sustained losses of circa 30% from peak prices, but I wasn't too dissatisfied, it was still an immensely profitable trade (when trend-following, a trader will rarely exit at the exact top of the market anyway). The credit crunch, as it came to be known, developed, and triggered one of the largest stock market falls ever. As the economy deteriorated more bad news was announced. Later that year a competitor slashed its profit forecast citing collapsing demand. Tanfield's share price slumped on the news. This was the first sign of trouble beyond the share price crashing, yet by this time the stock price had halved. Soon afterwards Tanfield released a series of profit warnings. The value of the company collapsed. Soon it was in financial difficulties.

Lesson Learned

Firstly, identifying stocks where the technical and fundamentals are both outstanding is not common, but it does occur. When identified, it pays to trade these opportunities very aggressively. The legendary hedge fund manager George Soros is renowned for saying 'When you're right you can't be right enough'. The basis for accumulating his $20bn fortune wasn't that he was right with a greater frequency than others, but that he identified several killer trades, betting very heavily on them.

Secondly, watch how a share price acts. Does it act stronger than the market or weaker? Has it changed the way it acts? This provides vital clues about the future prospects for a stock.

Thirdly, Tanfield's trade is an example of how daily checking of the list of stocks that are hitting 52 week highs and all-time highs frequently locates excellent stocks.

Fourthly, Tanfield expanded rapidly and this exposed the company to additional risks. In this instance the company undertook a series of acquisitions and then sought to consolidate production to achieve significant efficiency gains, which was an appropriate business strategy, since the company was in a very strong position with no debt. But although the fundamentals of Tanfield were excellent, when the economy deteriorated the large overheads of the new factory caused profitability to collapse. As the recession deepened losses mounted, causing crippling debts to accrue. Although the company survived the recession it was weak and was ultimately forced to sell a large share of the business cheaply. The company is now worth a fraction of its peak price. The lesson is that growth stocks normally outperform during good times, but rapid growth exposes companies to additional risks.

Fifthly, running profits is one aspect of trading that appears simple, but is actually difficult.

Finally, markets anticipate bad news. Experienced investors sold Tanfield stock knowing that a tightening of credit would impact the company especially hard. Traders familiar with technical analysis could see the signals of oncoming danger via the deterioration of the share price and the reversal in trend.

16 Betting Technique

Betting technique is the art of matching the amount of money risked to the potential of the trade, since a high probability trading opportunity will return no more than a standard opportunity unless the bet size is increased to correspond to the opportunity. It is also about the art of knowing when to exit a trade.

The accepted wisdom amongst traders is that no more than 3% of capital should be risked on any trade. I think that for beginners this is too high. New traders should approach trading cautiously and focus on conserving resources until they have profits. Once they have accumulated profits they should use this money to increase the size of the trades. For an excellent opportunity I risk up to 6% of trading capital per trade, targeting a gain of over 20%. For an average trade that doesn't set the pulse racing it is normally not worth risking more than 2%.

Good trading relies on probabilities and that means accepting the risk of loss on every trade. Experienced traders know that trading offers opportunities with varying probabilities, all except for certainty!

Modern society has accustomed us to very low error rates in our everyday lives. Businesses operate quality control systems such as the Six Sigma programme which targets an error rate of less than 1 in 1,000,000. But unlike advanced manufacturing processes, trading is not predictable and repeatable with high precision. It is as much art as science, making it tough for new traders to accept that errors occur even for traders of the highest standard. However, profitable trading can be achieved with error rates of 50% provided good betting techniques are applied. To do this each trade must receive commensurate financial backing relative to the grade of opportunity, with stop losses preventing significant losses and profits being allowed to flower.

Trading is much like the board game snakes and ladders. It takes many moves to progress up the board to the finish, with only a limited number of ladders which accelerate progress, but snakes exist that can send a player lower. The key to winning is not only to land on the ladders, but to avoid the perilous snakes that return the player to lower levels. With trading, as in the game, it is almost inevitable that on occasion we will land on a snake, causing significant regression. But trend-following using stop losses can help eliminate most large losses. A player who only has to slide down the snake a small distance has a much greater chance of winning the game than a player who slides all of the way to the bottom. The same applies to trading. Good betting techniques offer unlimited upside potential, but only limited downside losses, giving a greater chance of success.

	Trade A	Trade B	Trade C
Opening price	10.00	10.00	10.00
Target Price	13.00	11.50	11.00
Stop loss	9.70	9.50	9.50

Table 1. Some trades offering varying opportunities

Trade A offers the best opportunity, followed by trade B and then trade C. The quality of the opportunity is determined by the target price and the distance to the stop loss.

Several elite traders are former professional card players. This seems an unusual background for trading, but knowing the importance of betting techniques helps understand their success in the trading arena. Professional card players know that when holding good cards they must bet aggressively. In a weak position however they recognise that the best option is normally to exit the game. Professional card players do not get dealt a better hand than a novice player, nor do they expect to beat the novice player every time, good betting technique is the source of their success.

16.1 Setting the Target Price

How much to expect a share price to increase once it breaks out is always an estimate. Stocks with a high relative strength and strong earnings growth should be expected to rise the most. They have a strong tendency to move up in a series of legs higher, with trading ranges forming as the market pauses to consolidate gains. Examining how much the market moved on breaking out from its previous trading ranges provides a rough guide as to how much it will move higher on future legs upwards. Since earnings per share ultimately decides the share price, stocks with explosive earning growth and low P/E ratios often rise the quickest, especially if earnings are being frequently upgraded by analysts.

Lessons Learned

Firstly, betting technique enables the identification of favourable trades and is the cornerstone of all successful trading strategies.

Secondly, earnings per share growth rates, relative strength and previous price movements provide vital guidance on estimating future movements in prices.

Thirdly, each trader must discover what size trades they are comfortable with, and weight trades accordingly. Separating exceptional trading opportunities from the hum drum is critical to success, but regardless of how good a trade is, never risk more than your comfort level.

17. Trading Credit Cycles

The credit cycle has a huge influence on company earnings. This was demonstrated in a previous chapter, featuring Tanfield Plc, when contracting credit caused demand to plunge. Now let's look at the mechanism by which credit influences demand and company profitability using a simplified example:-

Person A earns £1000 per month, and also takes out a loan for £100 spending £1100 on work done by person B. Person B's income is £1100. Person B then takes out a loan for £100 and spends all of their income and the loan, totalling £1200 on work done by person C. Person C has an income of £1200 and takes out a loan for £100 and spends £1300. This simplified example shows how credit expands the economy, growing personal earnings and expenditure from £1000 to £1300.

Not only does the credit cycle influence the wealth of individuals, it can have an even more pronounced effect on company earnings. In our example of a mini economy consisting of 3 people, expanding credit grows spending from £1000 to £1300. Let's look at how a typical company's earnings would be affected by the credit expansion in our 3 person economy.

Our company has fixed costs such as rent (these costs don't vary according to output) of £750 and variable costs of £20 per £100 of goods production. Before credit expanded, the economy in our simplified example was £1000, so the company had revenue of £1000. Costs must be subtracted from revenue to determine profitability. Fixed costs are £750 and variable costs are 10 x 20 variable costs, giving total costs of £950. The company had revenue of £1000 minus fixed costs of £950 giving a profit of £50.

Now let's look at how the growth in demand that accompanies expanding credit influences profitability. Expanding credit means that the company's revenue has grown to £1300. Subtract from this fixed costs of £750 and variable costs of £20 per £100 produced, 13 x 20 = £260 of goods produced giving total costs of £750 + £260 = £1010. To calculate profits we must subtract total costs from revenue £1300 - £1010 = £290 profit.

The credit cycle has transformed the profitability of our company, with a profit increase from £50 to £290. A 30% increase in revenue causes profits to leap 580%. If we recall the outcome of Tanfield we now see how strongly profitability is influenced by the credit cycle. Therefore, when assessing a company it is vital to be aware of the credit cycle.

17.1 Banks and the Economy

During credit expansions the sense of wealth is enhanced giving increasing numbers of people the confidence to borrow money and banks the confidence to lend. Incomes rise and asset prices such as property and stocks normally increase. Banks enjoy good business, and loan defaults are low. Seeing that the economy is healthy and business is good banks make more loans. Increasing credit pushes incomes and asset prices higher.

The process of increasing lending creates a virtuous circle: Increased lending leads to increasing personal incomes, greater employment opportunities, rising company profitability and rising asset prices. But this cannot last because the economy has a finite capacity. When capacity is nearly reached businesses raise prices, causing increases in the prices of goods and services in the economy, workers then request pay increases. To prevent prices and wages spiralling ever upwards the central bank raises interest rates to stem the growth of new credit, hence slowing the economy. Credit slows, company profitability falls, many people's income falls, and asset prices slide, people lose their jobs and are unable to repay loans.

To prevent further losses banks restrict new loans, causing demand to continue to shrink. Falling demand leads to increasing spare capacity which causes the central bank to reduce interest rates. The interest burden on loans is reduced and people and businesses enjoy lower monthly repayments, giving a greater amount of disposable income which helps the economy to stabilise and begin to grow. Seeing the economy recover improves confidence and the credit cycle starts expanding again.

How much the profitability of a company is influenced by the credit cycle depends on the business. The profits in sectors such as homebuilding and construction are tightly linked to the credit cycle. These sectors are cyclical. The best time to invest in cyclical sectors is often during a recession or shortly afterwards when profits are depressed and the outlook for the economy is unclear. It can be risky to buy them long into an economic expansion when the credit cycle is near its peak. Other companies such as Unilever and Procter and Gamble are minimally impacted by the credit cycle. They produce products such as washing powder and food that people don't significantly reduce spending on during a recession. These sectors are said to be non-cyclical.

Lessons Learned

Firstly, some companies are impacted greatly by small changes in revenue. As the credit cycle expands and contracts profitability fluctuates greatly.

Secondly, the actions of Central Banks can have an important impact on company earnings (we will look at this in more detail in a later chapter)

Thirdly, Credit cycles greatly influence economic performance. Remember, good years on the stock market usually coincide with an expanding credit cycle, followed by tougher years when interest rates have been increased and the economy slows or tips into recession.

Finally, different companies are impacted by the credit cycle by differing amounts

18. Uncertainty

'Making great trades is hard, avoiding dumb trades is easy'

Charlie Munger - Billionaire investor

The credit crunch of 2008 sent markets into a tailspin. Economies around the globe fell into recession as credit contracted. In anticipation of the crash ending I was trying to figure out what products would be in demand when the current turbulence ended. I calculated that metals such as copper and iron ore would enjoy rebounding demand, and maybe hit new record high prices once the current crisis abated because the Chinese economy, which was the main consumer of metals, was still growing remarkably strongly. With many stocks priced at discounts of 80% or more compared to prices just 6 months ago, the mining sector looked devilishly attractive.

I reasoned that if I didn't invest too heavily in the mining sectors I could wait out any further turbulence until the credit cycle started a new upswing. The current prices of mining stocks were so low that I was unlikely to lose money in the medium to long term, but if the market recovered fully I would earn at least 200% profit, giving the trade an attractive risk reward ratio. Provided that I ignored the short term fluctuations of the market I felt certain that this was an opportunity to earn big money.

I questioned myself as to why I shouldn't take the plunge right now. It seemed like a good trading plan but the problem was that two key indicators, both of which were valid, were conflicting. Important valuation metrics screamed to buy, whereas every technical indicator said not to; prices were still in a downtrend. I interpreted these signals as showing the risk of short term losses was high because the trend was lower, but the probability of excellent long term gains was also high, because stock valuations were very attractive.

As the market slid lower I was relieved to have not invested. But then the market reversed and surged higher. Two gremlin voices in my head argued vigorously with each other about whether to buy. One, sensing that the market was getting away, saying that I was about to miss a great opportunity to buy, the other reasoned that market confidence takes many months to build before the market can sustainably recover and that this was probably just a market bounce that often occurs following a large drop in the market. Confident that the shares were so cheap that I couldn't lose over the long term I purchased a large quantity of mining stocks. I was now committed to being patient. I had to switch the trading brain off, and wait.

The market continued to rally, the tone of the market became increasingly positive. I became worried that I was underinvested. The gremlin in my head wanted to get more involved now, "Buy! Buy! Buy!" it howled, "You can't lose if you hold onto them, you might never get another chance and having seen such a great opportunity you will never be able to forgive yourself". The market was rallying hard and everyone seemed to be buying. I bought again, this time setting a tight stop loss to provide a justification for the trade. If I was exposed to a loss of only 5% then I could rationalise the trade, since it limited potential losses. The rally grew stronger. The media yap yaps on CNBC and Bloomberg were chattering away, excitement built in the market that the dark days of the bear market were over, and valuations were compelling. Of course, it didn't last and soon the market was diving again. The lovely positive tones of blue that had filled the profit column on my account flipped red. Only a few days ago traders were looking upwards, wondering how high the market would go, now we were all looking down and seeing a cavernous void. Thoughts of just holding stocks for the long term evaporated quickly, the viciousness of the plunge reminded me of what a foolish trade it had been. It was a mad dash for the exit as the market turned into a mudslide, selling everything.

Stocks that I had thought were great value at a 70% discount to their prior highs lost a further massive chunk of their value, with many losing another 75%. I had been harshly reminded that what you need for a great trade is for technical analysis and fundamental analysis to both be giving strong buy signals. I had been worried that the market would turn and rally higher leaving me under invested and missing out on some of the cheapest stocks I had ever seen. That fear had cost me, but this refresher lesson in trading came at an opportune time.

Having just had my fingers burned meant that avoiding making further impulsive trades was easy. I watched the market plunge, then make several other violent plunges lower. But then, although the market was volatile its movements over the coming months didn't leave it any lower. It was thrashing about, but had found a floor. Was the birth of a new uptrend pending? I was unencumbered with any losing positions; all resources were available to invest. I was free to cherry pick the market if it recovered. With hindsight I saw that exiting the market quickly on the previous trades might have been my best trading decision ever. It enabled the possibility to buy stocks at a fraction of the price I considered bargains just a few months ago.

Lessons Learned

Firstly, technical indicators trump fundamental indicators: During bear markets stocks often fall to ridiculously cheap valuations so buying based on valuation alone can lead to large losses.

Secondly, position yourself: making great trades is simpler when the trading account isn't filled with losing trades. If I hadn't have exited my losing trades I wouldn't have been able to summon the emotional strength to face investing everything when the market next signalled buy because carrying trades with heavy losses diminishes a traders abilities to function optimally.

Thirdly, don't let one mistake lead to another: If the bad decision to enter the market hadn't been reversed I wouldn't have attained the superb position that I found myself in. In short, position yourself; if you are not in a good position then get out of it quickly!

Fourthly, if you make one mistake don't let it lead to others. Reverse it immediately.

Fifthly, experience makes it easier to make the right choices: I was able to take the losses quickly because I could recall the emotional pain that carrying potentially large losses causes, and how it destroys the ability to trade effectively.

Sixth, the brain has two systems, one which acts emotionally and impulsively and another that reaches a judgement more slowly and is based on reasoning. When a trading opportunity has some very attractive attributes but doesn't fully meet requirements for investing it is more difficult to deny the impulse to trade. Impulsive trades are normally losing trades.

Finally, when profits turn to losses it is often a great signal that trades should be exited.

19. Trader Vic's Advice

'Where Fortunes Are Made: Identifying a Change of Trend'

Trader Vic, Methods of Wall Street Master

Many years had passed since first reading in Trader Vic's book [3] that fortunes were made identifying the change of trend, yet I had never forgotten it. That was probably because it sounded profound, but also because I thought it an exaggeration. I had doubted a trader could earn fortunes solely through identifying the change of trend, but stock prices had plunged following the credit crunch and caused the near collapse of the banking system. If a trader could call the end of this downtrend and the commencement of a new bull market then fortunes would be made, just as Trader Vic said.

This chapter is about how I identified that the market was changing from a vicious downtrend into a new uptrend, and focuses on one trade in particular to show how to recognise the most important thing a trader can learn – how to recognise the change in trend direction.

19.1 Identifying The Change of Trend

It starts when I identified a fragment of evidence that signalled something worthy of investigation. In the market meltdown of 2008/2009 I estimated the probability of encountering a mining company that was increasing in value as being as likely as meeting Elvis in the supermarket. An article in an investment magazine noted that several directors of a uranium mining company had purchased shares in another uranium explorer called Kalahari Minerals. My first thought was that the directors were foolish to invest new money in exploration companies because mining stocks were experiencing the most intense of selling pressure. But my next thought was that maybe the directors hadn't suffered a bump on the head, maybe they knew something. I decided to investigate.

The first piece of information examined was the share price chart. A look at the multi-year stock chart for Kalahari Minerals: where it's been, and where it's going - a chart really is worth a thousand words. Kalahari's stock chart conveyed the power of the buying interest in the stock. Global stock markets were down 40%, yet this stock was up 70%. It was a telling sign of specialness. The company website contained news about the company's operations. Its exploration program had been outstandingly successful, but only a small section of a 10km long section of rock, the focal point of the company's exploration effort, had so far been explored. All of this 10km section could contain high grade uranium. The signs were strong that the company was in the early stages of making a huge discovery.

The company website highlighted the presence of a world class uranium mine adjacent to the exploration acreage controlled by Kalahari, with several other large uranium mines located in close proximity. To the experienced eye this was important. The greatest chances of exploration success occur when near other major deposits, since natural resources are often found in clusters. My question as to why the directors were purchasing shares had been answered quickly.   Finding such an outstanding opportunity triggered the desire to immediately buy, but more rational thoughts intervened. This was not a market to be a buyer of stocks since the signal hadn't been given of a new bull market. Only a few months earlier, lured by attractive valuations, I had bought shares and lost money. The pain from this failed trade remained large making it easy to wait for the market's signal. The new leaders in the bull market would announce themselves when the new uptrend blossomed. I knew the signals, but had to be disciplined, and not make the same mistake again.

Although I didn't know exactly what the stock market would look like when a new bull market started, I mentally constructed an outline of the key signals confirming its occurrence. As a first signal, the downtrend must cease and markets must trade in a sideways range for at least 5 months, since major trends infrequently change direction quickly. The next phase would be for a group of strong stocks to trade above their 200 day moving average for several weeks, and stock prices to start new uptrends. I expected Kalahari and a handful of other stocks which had strongly resisted the selling pressure to be in this group, and then for them to lead the new bull market higher. That would be the final signal that the market had established a new bull market; it would then be time to buy.

Over the coming months Kalahari made a series of announcements detailing excellent drilling results. On each occasion the share price leapt, only to slowly retreat again. The decision to wait was being vindicated. In the coming months Kalahari's drill results were exceptional, but the stock price still remained boxed in, unable to escape its trading range. A picture formed in my mind of the grisly conditions in the stock market acting as a pressure cooker, containing Kalahari's stock price. The excellent drill results were building pressure for the stock to move higher, but investor apprehension about the economy was containing the price. My belief was, when the market was ready, Kalahari's price would explode higher and the stock would establish itself as a market leader.

I felt certain that we were in a long term bull for commodities, and the current sell off was a temporary interruption. Bull markets in commodities often last approximately 12 years and it is not unusual for them to include at least one period of crashing prices. Commodities started their run higher in 1999 and it was now 2008, so I reasoned that we might have several more years left before the end of the commodity cycle and this was likely to prove an excellent buying opportunity. If correct, commodity related sectors such as mining and oil exploration would lead the market higher again. The choicest stocks would have withstood the difficult times with the least damage. As an analogy, I viewed the market as an athletics competition, I wanted to select the athletes that were in the best shape to perform. I didn't want to be placing major bets on injured competitors whose performance would be handicapped by heavy debt loads or inefficient management. The excellent relative strength of Kalahari told me that the stock was in great shape, confirming my opinion that the company had excellent prospects.

I formulated a trading plan, if the market embarked on a major new uptrend my largest investment would be Kalahari stock. Consequently, I monitored the news closely, and was delighted by the progress. The news flow got better and better. The most recent press releases from the company stated:-

"Major hits on the southernmost line of Zone 1 give strong indication that this zone is still wide open. Rossing South (Kalahari's exploration project) is presenting both high grades and excellent widths, our progress since the initial discovery in February has been outstanding."

On reading the news release I immediately noted the terms "outstanding" and "excellent". These are unequivocal terms – company directors aren't looking for wiggle room when they use these terms to communicate with shareholders. Mud is clearer than terms which frequently populate shareholder communications. Words are often used such as "encouraging" - which, when spoken to shareholders is often director speak for disappointing, but better than nothing. In contrast, the terminology of the words "excellent" and "outstanding" are unequivocal. When these words are used they are often precursors to more good news – and this instance was to be no exception. On the 11th December 2008 Emerging Metals Plc, a small mining company controlled by billionaire mining mogul Stephen Dantels, purchased a large stake in Kalahari. (It's worth remembering, that at this time, there were literally thousands of small mining companies selling at bargain prices). Dantels was an investor with global scope, so his decision to invest in Kalahari gave me great confidence in the company's prospects.

By early 2009, signs of a stabilisation in the broader stock market were strong. By this time several other companies had purchased large blocks of Kalahari shares. There were many things that I didn't understand about mining and geology, so it was comforting to shadow their expertise. The intense desire of other mining companies to buy stakes in Kalahari made me certain that when the time came to invest in the market Kalahari would be the largest investment I would make. That's because the buying of stakes by other mining companies provided compelling evidence that Kalahari had unearthed an excellent mining resource, and that the price at which the stock was currently trading significantly undervalued Kalahari's discovery.

As 2009 progressed stocks established new uptrends, breaking out above previous resistance levels and trading above their 200 day moving averages, with the mining sector leading the market upwards. Technical analysis gave its long awaited buy signal and valuations were extremely cheap. My thoughts were in synchrony with the market, confirming that I was reading the markets signals correctly. I knew that when this happened I was rarely wrong in my forecasting. The more that I looked at the market the more I saw increasing signs that a new bull market in stocks and commodities was emerging. I couldn't find a single piece of evidence that signalled to wait any longer. The time to buy had arrived.

This was the kind of moment that made trading so good. The work was done and the decision made to go in big. Profits from the previous bull market had been preserved, bar the occasional loss. There was no route map of certainty for what the next few months would hold, but I sensed the market was filled with opportunity. All of the signals were green. I needed to succeed at this endeavour and to do so I had to invest aggressively when stock valuations and technical analysis both gave strong buy signals. It is obvious logic that the largest trades be placed on the best opportunities. On a scale of 1-10 I judged this opportunity to be as close to a 10 as any I had ever seen. More important than making money was avoiding a crippling loss that would impair future trading, so every position had a stop loss set at no more than 6% below the entry point. If the trades didn't work out, my wealth along with my confidence would be damaged, but it wouldn't be critical. In my heart, if I did eventually fail, I needed to know I'd maximised every opportunity and used every skill I had, and that meant really gunning at the best opportunities.

It was make or break for me in my ambition to become a successful trader and this was one of the moments Trader Vic was referring to when he said fortunes could be made by spotting when the market changes trend. I figured the present opportunity was so outstanding that it was a good time to break some trading rules. I went ahead and invested everything, plus leverage was used to moderately increase upside exposure.

Kalahari's stock price rocketed higher. When the company issued excellent drilling results the stock broke out on very heavy volume to a new all-time high. The other mining and oil exploration stocks that I had invested in also broke out, many on heavy trading volume. Technical analysis had enabled me to predict the breakout in stocks perfectly. Moreover, analysis of relative strength had correctly signalled that the mining sector would be the leading sector in the new bull market. Having identified many of the best stocks in the leading sector all that had to be done was avoid snatching profits too early. Patience would be now be the key to success.

I knew that negative news stories would continue to swirl and that the media, having been wrong so many times before, would be slow to recognise the change in the markets direction. The general consensus among traders and investors was also negative. They expected the rally to fail in much the same way as the preceding rallies had failed. The fact that so many traders were negative was one of the main reasons why I felt the market would move significantly higher since, as the market moves higher, they would need to re-invest, forcing the market upwards and drawing more money into stocks as other investors became desperate to buy. I remembered the market in 1987 and 2000 when traders exuded confidence, and how the high levels of confidence had marked the top of the market. I therefore reasoned that the extreme levels of pessimism currently present indicated that we were at the bottom of the market, and that a very large amount of upside existed. Whatever I read in the media, or whatever other traders said, whether they were highly regarded or not, I had to stay with the trend until the trend changed direction. It felt a lonely place to be. Every penny of trading capital I possessed was invested, yet few people seemed to conceive much possibility that we were on the cusp of a major new bull market.

Mining stocks led the market higher with Kalahari proving to be a runaway leader. Investors flocked back into the market as they desperately bought stocks that only a few months ago they had discarded.

Fig 23. *Kalahari Plc Breaking Out, Forming a New Uptrend*

After months of waiting it felt good to have big profits on the trading account, and the bull market was still young and fresh. The average time that a bull market lasts is approximately 3 years. For the first time in a long while I felt confident that much more profit would be forthcoming.

The drilling results from Kalahari continued to exceed expectations. Six months after breaking out the stock price had quadrupled to £2.00. But then, mysteriously, the ascent of the share price stalled despite continuing excellent drill results. I was at first unconcerned, since stock prices rarely increase in a straight line, but the stagnation continued for almost 6 months. During this time several attempts to push the stock price higher were met by sufficient selling to rebuff the advance. The price performance of Kalahari's stock was now subdued despite awesome drill results. Counter to expectations the stock then moved sharply lower whilst the rest of the market powered higher. This was not good, Kalahari had been left behind, but the reason was unknown. Searching the internet led to the discovery of rumours that the Russians were trying to gain control of Kalahari's project. It appeared that a rift had developed between Kalahari and the Namibian government. The

Russians had noticed the problems and had submitted a plan to the Namibians for Russian mining companies to work with the newly formed Namibian state uranium exploration company to take over Kalahari's project and develop the mine. Were the Namibians and the Russians going to seize control of Kalahari's assets? Had the Namibians formed the state company with the specific purpose of nationalising Kalahari's gigantic uranium project? Had Kalahari discovered a prize that was too big for the Namibians to allow foreign investors to take?

The Russians had a reputation for having scant regard for international law. They had been in the media for seizing control of large oil and gas projects owned by foreign companies on Russian territory. They had done this by alleging various breaches of the exploration licence. All mineral exploration licenses contain general clauses stating that the company must not harm the environment and that any significant discoveries must be developed within a reasonable time. Nationalisation of Kalahari's project could occur by citing breaches of these clauses. Even if the allegations were fictitious they would be difficult to categorically refute, and only one breach would be sufficient for Kalahari to lose control of the mine.

The cause of the divide between Kalahari and the Namibians was allegedly about how the project should be developed. The Namibians wanted Kalahari to commence mining operation immediately, thus generating jobs and wealth for the country. But from Kalahari's viewpoint, the optimal mine development plan could not be determined until the scale of the deposit was known.

I was dumbfounded by the number of things that could go wrong when investing in the stock market. After the difficulties of navigating through a collapsing world economy, then selecting the right stocks, and correctly timing entry into the market, I was now encountering problems because the project was so successful and so large! Who could have foreseen this problem coming? And were the Namibians and the Russians going to make a move to seize control, or was it just a rumour? Who knew? Who could tell?

Research confirmed that Namibia enjoyed close ties with Russia. Namibia is one of the largest and least densely populated countries in the world, with significant natural resources, and it was sensible for the Namibians to ally with Russia because of their defence capability which could be used to ward off aggressive neighbours wanting to acquire the precious natural resources. In the recent past the Russians had helped Namibia to win independence from South Africa and the two countries had enjoyed close relations ever since.

More Googling revealed another relevant fact. Namibia is rated one of the least corrupt countries in the world and mining companies were prepared to invest large amounts of money in Namibia because they trusted they would see a return on their investments and that contracts would not be changed and investments appropriated at the whim of government officials. Were the Namibians really going to sacrifice this hard-won international reputation? If the Namibians and the Russians seized Kalahari's assets on spurious grounds it would trigger an exodus of foreign investment from Namibia. The resultant draining of technological skills and capital would weaken Namibia, damaging its long term prospects. For these reasons, I didn't think the Namibians would seize the mine, but I was acutely aware that I was guessing the outcome.

The investment in Kalahari had deteriorated into a high stakes game of poker, and I didn't know the odds. To stick with Kalahari stock or fold, that was the question. To continue playing blind was not an option, the trade on the Kalahari was too big. The £40,000 trade in Kalahari was currently worth over £120,000. To wake up tomorrow and have lost it all would be awful, yet not without possibility. The share price was continuing its slide and was now trading below critical technical indicators. The 200 day moving average had turned lower, indicating that investors were exiting the stock on a sustained basis. I needed to make a decision.

I thought back to when I had originally bought this stock. I had identified the trade by following the money, but now the money was dashing for the exit; should I follow? It brought me to thinking, maybe the Namibians were bluffing, using the threat of partnership with the Russians to force Kalahari into a compromise. This made sense. But believing that I understood the situation, and actually understanding the situation were different: the risks remained. Reluctantly, I had to sell the stock. Pulling the trigger and exiting the stock hurt. It really, really hurt.

A week after selling and Kalahari stock was rocketing skyward again. I repurchased some shares as the price motored higher, but I didn't want to get caught holding a significant shareholding because uncertainty remained. The stock soon doubled in value in just a few months. Then Kalahari received a takeover bid, boosting the price further. The possibility of a bidding war arose. I was disappointed I didn't own more stock, but worse things happen in life.

Then, on the 11th March, 2011 a disaster occurred. Japan was struck by a huge earthquake followed by several tidal waves. Thousands of people died and the Fukushima nuclear plant was damaged. A notable risk I had identified prior to investing in uranium stocks was that a major nuclear accident at a power plant would occur, stirring public opposition to nuclear power and curtailing the growth of the industry. I'd examined how the nuclear accident at Chernobyl years earlier had impacted the value of uranium mining companies, most uranium stocks lost at least 70% of their value. I also assessed the frequency of major nuclear incidents; they didn't happen very often, but I recalled noticing the absolutely abysmal safety record of the Japanese nuclear industry. Moreover, I had noticed several reports detailing how the Japanese nuclear industry had repeatedly concealed the severity of accidents at their nuclear power plants.

When the Fukushima incident occurred and the news reports stated it was a serious, but contained incident, I was sceptical. I needed to sell Kalahari stock immediately, before the full extent of the tragedy was revealed. As I logged onto my computer I braced myself for bad news. Would uranium stocks be down 30%, 50% or even more I wondered? Would I even be able to sell, or would the market be saturated? As the share price quotes started to appear on the screen I shut both eyes and faced the computer, took a deep breath, drew the air in from my nose and edged one eye open to peek at the stock quotation. I was amazed, the average losses in the uranium mining sector were only 5%. My eyes popped wide open as I made a dash to sell the shares. I was as sure as I had ever been that the news about the Fukushima disaster was going to hit my trading account hard. I'd dodged a bullet.

Over the next few weeks the news got worse as the full extent of the tragedy was exposed. Nations around the world announced curtailed nuclear power programs and some nations revoked their programs completely. With long term demand for uranium slumping, the uranium price collapsed. The price of uranium mining stocks also slumped, with most losing 50% or more of their value in just a few weeks.

A major opportunity had been missed. I should have immediately sold short uranium mining companies, enabling profits to be made from the slump in the uranium sector. Mark Twain said that history doesn't repeat itself, but it rhymes. In this instance history provided a perfect melody for the song to be played. I knew the song, but I didn't sing. I was too worried about being wrong.

My research had strongly indicated that the Japanese would downplay the incident, meaning the market would be slow to realise the truth. Also, the market seemed unfamiliar with the story of what impact a significant nuclear accident would have on the uranium sector. History had provided the perfect template to aggressively short sell uranium stocks. What I couldn't fathom was why I didn't act with greater venom. I figured I was relieved at selling the Kalahari shares I held without incurring heavy losses. As I mulled the missed opportunity I was struck by the realisation that this was one of the first instances in my trading career where I knew the history, I knew the market, I had the edge, and I was one of the guys who should have led the market and applied the selling pressure to the uranium miners and cleared a fast 50% profit in a very short space of time.

Like a boy coming of age, the ability was present, but confidence and concentration on the game wasn't.

I vowed….next time…

Lessons Learned

Firstly, when you have an edge in the market trade aggressively.

Secondly, it wasn't necessary to be an expert geologist to make large profits from Kalahari stock. The ability to trade confers the ability to trade almost any stock, regardless of knowledge about the underlying business (although I do prefer to know as much as possible).

Thirdly, unforeseen occurrences offer the small trader opportunities because they can act quickly, meaning they beat larger traders to the opportunity.

Fourthly, identifying a change of trend really is the single most important skill that a trader can acquire; it really is where fortunes are made. The larger the trend that is changing direction, the better the opportunity.

Fifthly, history provides invaluable insights. In this instance, knowing about the impact of past nuclear accidents provided invaluable insights.

Finally, sometimes horrific things happen. Being a professional trader requires detachment from emotionally upsetting events.

With the exception of Kalahari the investments in mining and oil exploration stocks boomed. The average length of a bull market is over 3 years. Knowing this prevented me hastily taking profits. Holding onto excellent trades provided they perform as expected is all that needed to be done to earn very large profits as the global economy boomed and markets recovered strongly.

20. Reading the Market

Between 1999 and 2008 oil prices increased spectacularly, rising from $20 to over $140 per barrel. When the stock market crashed in 2008 the price of oil had slumped, but the world economy was now recovering and the price was surging higher again. The rocketing oil price caused a corresponding increase in the stock prices of oil exploration companies and a surge in new exploration activity. But despite this, the increase in new oil discoveries remained disappointing.

According to the text books this shouldn't happen. High prices should cause a surge in exploration and new oil discoveries. However, oil had particular circumstances that suggested finding new oil would not be cheap or easy. The primary factor was that the only areas unexplored were remote corners of the world, meaning that exploration would be complex and expensive.

One such region was the Falkland Islands, located just 850 miles north of the Antarctic Circle. Geologists had long ago noticed the Islands were composed of an abundance of rock containing the remnants of trapped plant and fossil material from which oil is generated. The British Geological Survey estimated that this source rock could have produced as much as one hundred billion barrels of oil. This, combined with seismic data showing suitable rock formations where the oil could have become trapped, suggested that the geology was suitable for making world class oil discoveries. Years earlier Shell had carried out exploration work, proving the existence of a working petroleum system, but exploration halted when the oil price fell, rendering exploration unviable. It seemed logical that Shell's preliminary search marked the beginning and not the end of oil exploration in the region.

But oil exploration in remote regions is challenging and expensive, with suitable oil rigs costing $250,000 per day to hire, and long waiting times. To improve their chances of securing a rig, a consortium was formed by several Falkland Island exploration companies. Eventually a rig was secured and exploration could commence.

I thought the rationale that the waters around the Falklands may contain oil compelling, and, provided the oil price stayed high, I wanted to invest. Having never invested in an oil company before I was unsure how to select the best shares from the many Falkland exploration companies that were listed on the stock market. I decided to rely on the market's indications since it would signal the opinion of knowledgeable investors.

Desire Petroleum's stock price had outperformed the other Falklands' exploration stocks, meaning it had the highest relative strength of all the Falkland's exploration stocks. This was the market's signal that this stock had the highest probability of success. Additionally, the stock met most of my other investment criteria. It was in a leading sector, and the price was trading above its 50 and 200 day moving average. The company wasn't profitable, but it did have a rapidly expanding inventory of quality exploration targets, which I accepted in lieu of growing earning per share as evidence that this was a growth stock.

When the company commenced making rental payments for the rig the race to strike oil got underway as the companies were now burning through their funds. The thought of finding billions of barrels of oil generated a buzz of excitement amongst investors as Desire Petroleum took control of the rig and sunk the drill bit into the rock. Drilling the first target was expected to take 30 days. Because of the positioning of the first two drilling targets, both could be tested with a single probe of the drill, since they were buried deep in the rock, stacked on top of one another.

To ensure I kept abreast of the latest developments and was aware of the necessary documents and research I routinely followed several knowledgeable bloggers on an internet bulletin board. Some bloggers, with names like Offshore Hero and Oil Brat were employed in oil exploration. Other highly knowledgeable posters didn't have a background in oil exploration, but had superb research skills and flexible mind-sets that enabled them to perform a professional analysis of the information. As a novice to oil exploration the bulletin board proved to be a useful forum for learning about the subject, with people referencing important geological documents and sharing knowledge.

20.1 The First Drill

As the first drill approached target depth the excitement on the bulletin board increased. Tens of thousands of small investors visited the bulletin board every day, reading the latest news and opinions, and expressing their own thoughts. Some investors posted that they thought the stock was worth 5 times the current price, others devised calculations that justified even higher levels of upside potential. Just days before investors were expecting news on whether the drilling had been successful, a newspaper published an article claiming that the drill had already reached its target, and that the well contained only traces of oil. Speculation was ignited on the bulletin board about whether the newspaper article was factually correct. Had the journalist received false information to cause the stock price to fall, enabling others to move in and buy the stock at depressed prices? Investor speculation grew rampant, so the company issued a statement. Unfortunately it revealed the newspaper article was correct. Drilling had found only traces of oil. Nonetheless, the company had five more prospects to test, and this was only the first round of drilling, so it wasn't a major setback.

Given the large number of remaining prospects I estimated the price may drop as much as 25%. But then came the real shock. Just before the market opened the stock was indicated to decline 70%. It was carnage, no rational explanation existed for such a thunderous drop. As I read the posts on the bulletin board a trader had written 'no oil means no market cap justification' implying that without oil the company couldn't justify its current value. From all the thousands of posts, these few words summarised the situation with unparalleled succinctness. Prior to the results the company was valued at £300million; such a lofty valuation was extremely vulnerable to bad news. The technical indicators to which I had paid so much attention when making the investment really meant nothing.

If there was no oil, the stock was worthless. My heart sank as I realised the mess I was in.

I had veered a very long way from the stock selection criteria that had previously been successful. When I reconsidered my holding of Desire Petroleum I couldn't help but wonder if I had bought into a stock when its price was frothy with excitement, much like 10 years earlier when internet stocks had experienced highly inflated valuations as investors became giddy with enthusiasm about their future.

Mulling over the present situation caused me to question my investment. After all, what did I really know about oil exploration? And where was my edge over the competition? It was too late now, I was going to suffer hurtful losses. That morning, when the stock market re-opened for trade, the price cratered on very heavy volume. The losses triggered reflection on the trade, and I realised that my initial rationale for making the trade was weak. I had calculated that if I used a stop loss located 20 % below the share price then I would gain unlimited upside potential, but limited downside exposure. Because the market gapped lower, with trading starting at a price 60% lower than the previous day's price the stop loss was useless because no trading took place at that price where my stop loss was located. I now faced a dilemma. Did I sell on the basis that the price was below the stop loss even though I thought the current price too cheap? For the first time in many years I decided against selling even though the stop loss level had been breached. With my usual indicators of relative strength, trend information and stop loss points all abandoned, I had none of my usual bearings which I used to navigate the market; I was like a ship lost at sea.

In desperation I headed back to the Desire Petroleum bulletin board. Maybe somebody knew something - maybe there would be a post that supported my view point, since I felt all hope had been lost prematurely. But the previously jovial atmosphere on the bulletin board had degenerated into a witch hunt against the optimistic, with traders who had previously expressed confidence in the stock being humiliated. Old posts where people had expressed optimism were fished out, and the authors named and shamed, highlighting their foolishness. Other traders clicked the like button to show support for those doing the humiliation. Even posters who had previously provided constructive information that was free of personal opinion were accused of being foolish.

The leading supporter of the case for finding oil in the Falklands was a trader who used the pseudo name 'Garbled'. He bore the brunt of the jibes about how misguided traders had become in thinking there was oil in the seas around the Falklands. In his defence he referred to posts where he had stated that the stock was worth £20 or 20p, and to reflect his ambiguity about the company's prospects Garbled proceeded to give his new price forecast as unchanged at £20p. The £20p forecast was an adept summation; the coming drills would result in a stock price of £20 or 20p. With my stop loss abandoned I had relinquished control, and boarded the £20p roller-coaster.

With the next drill result due in only 3 days the bulletin board's lynch mob became more cautious with their berating since they would be the fools if oil was found. The bulletin board was split on the prospects for success. Most were hoping for oil, but a growing number of traders were shorting the stock, sensing that the stock price was still too expensive.

20.2 The Next Drill

Geologists believed this drill to have a lower chance of success. It was selected primarily because the distance between the previous drill target and this target was small. They were stacked on top of one another, it was just a matter of continuing to drill through the previous target to reach this one. The share price gained as the drill neared its target. Although the stock's value was still much lower than when I had bought, I used the significant bounce in the share price to dispose of a large portion of my stockholding. The following day the result of the drill was released. It showed only traces of oil. The share price skidded lower once again.

Many investors who had held onto their shares, and some of those who had used the fall in the price to increase their holdings posted stories about their heavy losses on the bulletin board. Some lost their savings, others slid into financial difficulties, putting pressure on their personal relationships. They had become cocooned in the reassurance and excitement of the bulletin board group and with so many positive and supportive posts being made, as well as friendships and trust being formed, they had risked too much. Undoubtedly some competition between traders was also to blame, with people posting contract notes showing how many shares they had bought to prove their commitment and belief in the exploration project, and also as a show of wealth and bravado. The need to not be the trader who missed out on the spoils of a big oil discovery meant some had become blinded to risk; only now was the folly of their actions apparent. Everyone was searching for answers, trying to reason out what to do next. But reason relied on facts, and nobody knew if the coming drills would yield oil. It was a matter of enduring the uncertainty or selling out.

20.3 Rockhopper's Drill

The rig moved to a new exploration area operated by Rockhopper Exploration plc to drill a new well called Sea Lion. Geologists thought the chances of success here were lower than on the previous drills. As the drill neared target depth I began a series of early starts to check if pre-market news had been released, as important news is often released prior to the market opening, allowing traders time to digest it. Then the news came that we had all been waiting for. The drill results were announced, it was amazing news, Rockhopper had made a substantial oil discovery. The game was back on again. This was the signal to buy Rockhopper shares and repurchase shares in Desire Petroleum. These companies were no longer wildcatters taking longshots drilling in the vast expanses of the Southern Ocean, they'd found oil. An oil deposit located in total isolation is rare, others are normally nearby and so buying the moment the market opened would be wise. I planned to move quickly and get into the market before the big investment funds and hopefully watch the share price travel higher for the next few days as the big players bought stock.

I bought seconds after the market opened, volume was already heavy. When the day's trading finished the share price had risen over 100% and closed the trading session near the highest price of the day. Volume was over 10 time's average. The explosive market action inclined me to believe that further increases in the stock's price were likely. I had to stay with the trend higher and not sell unless hard factual news was released which contradicted my opinion.

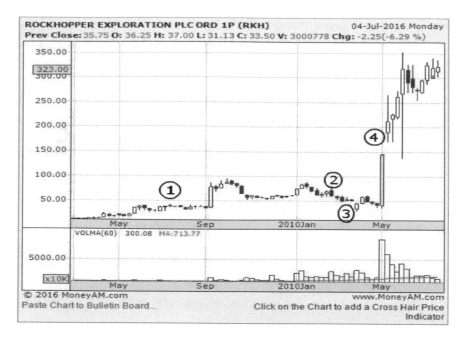

Fig: 24 *(Above) Rockhopper Exploration Breaks Out*

Technical Analysis of Rockhopper Exploration Plc

1. **The market trends higher, anticipating good news.**
2. **Profit taking prior to first drill results causes price to decline.**
3. **The price slumps 40% when the well drilled by Desire Petroleum is dry.**
4. **The price and trading volume explodes on the release of news of striking oil. The market continues to absorb the news, surging higher.**

On the 4th June, 2010 Rockhopper released additional news about its oil discovery at the Sea Lion prospect, saying 'every sand beneath the regional seal is charged with oil' and that the board believes 'a new regional fairway has been opened'. Having little geological knowledge, this meant nothing, but to the oil guys who posted on the bulletin board it was beautiful music. They said that the geological evidence now suggested that huge quantities of oil were sealed beneath rock, and that a long fairway of sandstone formations, most likely containing vast quantities of oil, had been found. The oil companies had a geological model explaining the basin and the oil's location. The billions of barrels of oil expelled from the nearby source rock millions of years ago hadn't oozed into the sea; it was trapped and its location was known.

Technical analysis of Desire Petroleum and Rockhopper signalled a highly positive outlook, with both stocks trading above their medium and long term moving averages and the stock price trending higher on very heavy trading volume. Fundamental analysis was also highly positive, with the realistic prospects of finding many world class discoveries. Everything suggested increasing the bet size would be lucrative.

I had earned very substantial profits, but it was unsafe, because much more work had to be done to prove that the oil could actually be extracted. The well needed to be flow tested. If the well failed this test much of the oil wouldn't be recoverable, and the share price would tumble. Once again I had to be ready act on news. Leaving the computer, even for a short time, could result in huge losses. Throughout the day I was never usually far from a computer anyway, but now I had to have a constant price quote for Rockhopper and Desire Petroleum on the screen, and be ready to quickly trade.

Meanwhile, on the bulletin board, excitement overflowed. The trader named 'Garbled' who had been one of the most vocal and confident supporters of the prospects of finding oil on the bulletin board led a merry band of ecstatic traders, elated by their success. They posted dealing notes showing their profits, and enjoyed their moment returning the public humiliation to those who had been so unkind to them when the previous drills didn't find oil. The Falkland Island explorers had nearly made the leap from exploration minnows into major league exploration and production companies. Many traders speculated that the big oil companies were preparing takeover bids to secure a stake in these major new oil fields, but everyone knew the bids wouldn't fly unless the flow test data was positive.

At 3.30 pm on 17 September 2010, the results were released. It was fantastic news. In moments the shares of both companies rocketed nearly 50%. We were ecstatic with joy; our shares were like winning lottery tickets. But this wasn't just a time for celebration, it was a time for action. I had to seize the moment and buy more shares, since a new oil basin had been found, and it was full of recoverable oil. If I didn't buy more I would have failed to fully maximise the opportunity. The mantra of the billionaire speculator George Soros rang in my ears 'when you're right, you can't be right enough'. Soros believed in aggressively building his position when the market told him that he was right and I intended to follow his mantra. We were in one of the biggest bull markets for commodity prices ever. I had over 15 years' experience in the market and was at the top of my game. This was a great opportunity; the only mistake now would be to not buy heavily.

20.4 The Next Drill

After completing the flow test the rig returned to Desire Petroleum. On account of new geological evidence from Rockhoppers drill, a new drill target called Rachel was chosen. It was situated along the migratory path that the geological model suggested the oil had flowed millions of years ago. The theory behind the Rachel drill was that geologists knew the location of the source rock and also that some of that oil had become trapped at the Sea Lion discovery, therefore they knew the route the oil had travelled. Seismic survey data had identified the giant rock formations along the route where the oil should have become trapped. If they were correct Rachel should be filled with oil, with billions more barrels located along the route. It would be the most important drill so far. The significance of the Rachel drill was highlighted by geologists on the bulletin boards. One of them, using the pseudo name Marlon Monkey posted:-

> 'Rachel is key. Whatever your strategy the Rachel result is key. The   regional fairway is what we are all in this for. This is a 6-10 billion-barrel fairway. Rachel is key.'

The drill at Rachel was a huge event, and the city stockbrokers weren't prepared to miss the feast. They published buy recommendation as they sought to generate trading commissions from the Falklands oil bonanza. One respected city brokerage published a note stating the next drill alone was worth up to 520p per share for Desire, compared to Desire's current price of 180p. Many other brokers published equally optimistic price targets. It was true that if the Rachel prospect held oil the geological code for the basin was unlocked and billions of barrels of oil would surely be found. The Falkland Islands would become the hottest oil exploration area in the world. The Rachel well, because of the information she would reveal and the quantity of oil she might hold, became the single most important oil well drilled in British waters for a generation.

In addition to drilling the Rachel prospect, the company announced it would explore new unchartered areas of the basin. The new seismic survey would focus on the flank of the basin nearest to Rockhopper's discovery. The results would not be known for many months, but it highlighted that vast areas of ocean remained unexplored.

Drilling started at Rachel. Soon the results were expected and the share prices of the Falkland Island exploration stocks exhibited strength, reflecting investor optimism. But something unexpected occurred. Desire's share price slid on heavy trading volume, a large investor taking profits I figured. I expected it wouldn't last; the price dip would be noticed and the unwanted stock bought. But I was badly mistaken, instead the stock price skidded violently lower. Soon it had dropped 10%, then 15% and still skidding, meanwhile trading volume bulged.

My trading senses told me that something serious was wrong. I urgently checked the company website, but no news. So I quickly scanned the bulletin boards, desperately looking for clues. Traders had posted about the unusual trading activity, but nobody offered a reason. However, one of the board's most knowledgeable posters, called Offshore Hero, said he had sold out, but gave no further details. Offshore Hero had contacts within the industry, he had posted words to that effect, but never elaborated. I wondered, was his post a hint, intimating that he knew something, but for fear of insider trading regulations couldn't post details. He'd never expressed any prior inclination to sell; he understood the geology, the risks, and the rewards. His post had to be a hint of new information.

There was no time for procrastination, the market closed shortly. I needed to decide whether to sell, but was worried the market might rebound the moment I sold, so I fudged the decision, selling only half. Only time would judge if I was correct. In the final moments of trading millions of shares flooded onto the market, it slumped to close at the very lowest price for the day, with the price tumbling over 20%. The market was signalling, in a way as clear as I had ever seen, that further moves lower would occur and that all shares should be sold as soon as trading started tomorrow.

The next day I breathed a sigh of relief when the market reopened. The price was stable and it even manged to nudge higher by a few pence. But I knew that it was often the case that traders who didn't know how to read the market would have noticed the price fall and think it an opportunity to buy some cheap shares. I hastily sold most of my remaining holdings. Once the bargain hunters had done their buying I expected the market to break lower again. If I was correct I would sell my few remaining shares on the first signs of the market folding over again. An hour into the trading session and the market began to crack as selling pressure overwhelmed the market. The plunge restarted and trading volume accelerated sharply as the sell-off gathered pace. I immediately sold the remainder of my stock. The share price tried to rally several times during its descent, but each time it was met with further waves of selling. What was going on? When would this stop? Had crucial news leaked out again?

I watched the panic grow. The selling wasn't abated by the falling price, instead it was like an avalanche; its force growing as the slide gathered momentum. By the close of trade Desires stock price was down forty percent. Trading volume was a whopping thirty times average, yet there was no news from the company. The power of the market's slide suggested that many people held insider information and that negative news was imminent. Unfortunately, I wasn't in the loop, instead the signals from the changes in price and trading volume warned me to sell. Inexperienced traders, like rabbits in the headlights, couldn't read the market's signals and sense the danger. The falling market crushed them.

At 7.20 am the next morning the company issued news. The drill hadn't found oil. But the company stated, "Based on the latest information from this well, potential sandstones have now been identified down deep from the existing location, closer to the mature oil source rock, significantly reducing the oil charge risk." As a result the well was to be diverted using a side track to a slightly different target. I immediately realised the suspense wasn't over, but had incomplete news leaked into the market that the well was dry? Was the market aware that they would be now be testing a slightly different zone? The only way to know the markets opinion was to watch its reaction.

When the market opened the price held firm; the bad news was already priced in, confirming that the drilling results had been leaked. The company's statement re-ignited debate on the bulletin boards about whether to buy or sell. The words from the news release by Rockhopper following the initial oil discovery, "all sands beneath the regional seal rock are charged with oil" were mentioned again and again on the bulletin board. People concluded that this statement had yet to be disproven. However, should the new side-track well fail nothing would be left to underpin the share price, because the geological model for the basin would be falsified, removing the rationale for Desire's current valuation of £300 million. The share price would crumble. Moreover, the stock was now trading below its 200 day and 50 day moving average and the price was in a down trend. There was no reason to invest.

On 12 November 2010 drilling on the side track well, named Rachel North, commenced. The results from the well were released a few weeks later. They had found oil. Commenting on the discovery, Stephen Phipps, Chairman of Desire said, "It is highly encouraging that the initial results from Rachel North endorse both our findings and geological model from the previously drilled Rachel well. This discovery combined with Rockhoppers' Sea Lion discovery confirms our belief that the eastern flank fairway in the North Falkland Basin is highly prospective and that further oil fields will be discovered in this area." With that the share price surged over 20%. The find wasn't as significant as some expected since the amount of oil found was small, but it kept the dream of making a huge oil discovery alive.

Shortly afterwards the company released more news, except this news was more scandalous than any of the prior shenanigans investors had thus far endured. I had to reread the statement several times, and then check the internet for confirmation that I was interpreting the news correctly, because the news was freakish. The statement implied that the Rachel North prospect wasn't full of oil as had been stated, it was actually full of water. I checked the company's share price, it was collapsing. At that moment I knew I had understood the news correctly. The company said that oil from its drilling operation had contaminated the sample, leading the company to believe that it had found oil, when really the drill only found water.

For me, and for many other private investors, the Falkland's saga, riddled with blatant insider trading activity, topped off with the 'it's water, not oil' scandal marked the end of the road for investing in small oil exploration companies. We had been on a journey of emotional highs and lows, to places where good investing shouldn't take you. I'd have to put this episode down to experience. Time to move on.

Lessons Learned

Firstly, some events that a company is exposed to are so important, yet also unknowable, that the usefulness of technical analysis in reading the market is minimal.

Secondly, large investment institutions can be slow to reallocate resources, leading to a stream of orders hitting the market for many days following the release of transformative news. Nifty traders can react speedily and profit by investing quickly and riding the ensuing wave of buying.

Thirdly, adding to a trade as a stock price rises is often a profitable trading method, but if the trend breaks down the pyramiding of trades must be reversed.

Fourthly, booms and bust recur. Each time they re-appear in a different guise. The boom in internet stocks was followed by a boom in commodities. Trading booms and bust often yields exceptional results. But remember, booms nearly always lead to busts because the high prices that accompany booms cause a dearth of new supply, precipitating the bust phase.

Fifthly, some stocks are a piñata, you don't know what they contain until a certain moment, and then all is revealed. These speculative stocks are best avoided, especially when using leveraged trades.

Sixth, I was self-employed during the time I was trading the commodities boom, so I had the flexibility to fit trading around other work commitments and monitor the markets closely when necessary. For traders without this flexibility they need to take into account how quickly they will be able to act when selecting which companies to trade, since the important announcements made by oil exploration stocks sometimes meant that time was of the essence, and not being able to trade because of work commitments could be an expensive hindrance.

Seventh, bulletin boards can occasionally be a useful source of information, but care has to be taken not to be unduly influenced by other people's opinions. In this instance many traders were influenced by the growing sense of euphoria and gained reassurance about their investment choices from others, leading to excessive risk taking.

Finally, this is an account of a trade that should make traders question what they really know when trading a situation. Company statements and the statements of politicians and central banks are often found to be untrue. Traders need to consider this when sizing their trades and positioning stop loss points since these factors are determined by the quality of the evidence which the trade is based upon.

21. In the Jungle

Dave Forest was the writer of the Pierce Point's newsletter, penning it as he travelled the world evaluating mining projects. He wrote about investing in the booming natural resources sector. From humble beginnings he studied the alchemy of turning moose pastures into mega mines and had succeeded in making his fortune in the mining industry. His keen eye and geological expertise enabled him to discover one of the largest gold deposits in the world, as well as other lucrative mining opportunities, making him a wealthy man. He shared his expertise with investors via his free newsletter, and, because commodities were hot, I was an avid reader.

He repeatedly highlighted coal as being a commodity in short supply. Valuations for the right mining project were surging as expert delegations from India and China competed to secure coal mining investments. I currently didn't hold shares in coal mining companies, but the explosive price moves screamed that getting involved could be very lucrative. All I needed to do was find the right stock.

There were only a few coal mining stocks traded on the London market, but one stood out, Churchill Mining Plc. The more I researched the company, the more it appealed. It exhibited so many similarities to other successful investments I had made that it was difficult not to get excited. The most important similarity was the persistent purchasing of Churchill's shares by other businesses who were in the coal mining and energy sector. Additionally, Churchill had already received several approaches to purchase all or part of the company's mining project. The evidence was all fitting together. At the present time coal was the in-demand commodity and Churchill

Mining was a very desirable company, capable of meeting the booming demand for coal from the emerging economies of China and India.

I plunged in and bought Churchill's shares. The stock price chopped about as the market was hit by concerns over the global economy, but the problems impacting the broader market appeared to be approaching resolution and the stock market powered to a new high with the mining sector strongly outperforming. The value of my portfolio surged, but there was a notable laggard; Churchill's stock price hadn't moved. Identifying the reason for the stock's soggy performance proved elusive. With concerns over the global economy fading I figured potential bidders who had previously built shareholdings would surely be poised to launch takeover bids. The market should be anticipating this and pricing the shares sharply higher, so what was the problem? There was a slim chance that there wasn't actually a problem. It could just be a large shareholder selling, temporarily swamping the market but I rated this an outside possibility. With my stock market experience leading me to think that perhaps something more sinister lay behind Churchill's underperformance I began viewing Churchill's stock suspiciously.

My fears lessened when the stock caught a bid and moved higher. Then Churchill issued news that its project had a Net Present Value (NPV) of over £1billion (the stock was currently valued by the market at only £200 million). The market embraced the news, marking the share price higher on heavy trading volume. All of the elements looked to be in place for the stock to blast past its all-time high price of 140p. But the stock price again faded, unable to sustain the move higher despite valuations in the rest of the mining sector marching briskly upwards. It was all about what the stock price didn't do that signalled something was amiss.

My suspicions increased when the company announced that it had received takeover approaches again. This caused the share price to surge, but once again it fizzled out, and it wasn't long before it had given back all the recent gains. This stock wasn't acting like that of a quality company in the midst of booming market; it seemed lifeless. But the reason why remained unanswered. A good place to start investigating was to re-examine the company's statement that its project had a Net Present Value of £1 billion. I was confident that sufficient time had now passed for expert investors in the mining sector to have evaluated this bold statement, and, judging by the poor stock price performance I figured most had sniggered at Churchill's lofty self-valuation.

I realised my ability to appraise the £1billion Net Present Value price tag Churchill had placed on itself was limited, since the calculation incorporated many specific costings to build and operate the mine, as well as the forecast selling price of the coal. It also included values for how much coal would be mined and an allowance for the cost of finance. I had no edge in performing these types of calculations, or estimating the correct value of each component, but I understood some basic facts.

If the project contained 2 billion tonnes of extractable coal and the company made £2 profit per tonne that approximated a value of several billion pounds. I also realised that because the mine was expected to produce huge volumes of coal, a small change in the assumed selling price of each tonne made a huge difference to profit forecasts, and hence affected the value of the project. It wasn't necessarily that Churchill's figures were incorrect, it was that a small change in coal prices caused large changes in the company's value. Whilst Churchill could legitimately place a high value on itself there was absolutely no assurance that it was attainable.

Investigating the Net Present Value yielded few clues as to why the share price was underperforming and I moved onto the other factor that was a nagging concern - why other companies who were thought to be interested in launching takeover bids had ceased accumulating Churchill's stock - since by this time many months had passed without any new takeover bids or stake building. Maybe potential bidders now believed the stock to be fully valued or, alternatively, they were aware of other problems. I didn't want to get caught holding a stock that was substandard. I was looking for stocks that other investors were identifying as screaming buys, ones where you got a real sense investors were desperate to buy the stock.

Using the maxim 'if in doubt get out', I was seriously considering selling-out, such thinking had served me well in the past. But before I followed my hunch I decided on one final check. I would look on the internet bulletin boards to see if any other ideas had been put forward for Churchill's disappointing performance that would be worthy of further research.

I was in luck. A blogger using the nickname 'Old Dynamite' had been busy blowing holes in the case for buying Churchill's stock. One pillar of his argument rested on the fact that the coal on Churchill's tenements had very high water content (almost 40%) meaning it had a much lower net energy value than some investors believed. Old Dynamite said the coal's energy value was 5200kcal/kg, but this was only attained after the coal had been through an intensive drying process. He implied that huge amounts of energy were necessary to dry the coal, meaning that the coals net energy would be much less than the 5200kcal.kg stated by the company, it was more likely close to 3250kcal.kg.

The blog emphasised that Churchill's reserves statement excluded mention of coal quality and this was probably a breach of requirements. A blogger using the nickname 'Valuta' immediately responded to Old Dynamite's attack, quoting a research document which stated that the coal in that region did in fact have an energy content of 5200kcal.kg., and had a comparable energy content to other thermal coals from Australia and Indonesia and was strongly sought after by Asian power producers. Old Dynamite replied that 'shysters and the untrained always quote the calorific value on an air dried basis because it is a bigger number' (as Churchill often did) and that Valuta should look at the net amount of energy that would be derived from the coal after drying. Perhaps tellingly, Valuta didn't respond. Old Dynamite asserted that the net amount of energy the coal yielded was so little that after the expense of mining, drying and transportation, its value on the Chinese or Indian market would be insufficient for Churchill to generate any significant profit. The coal had such a low net energy content it was only suitable if there was a nearby power station with a large local population to serve, which wasn't the case as Churchill's project was in a remote area. For Churchill's coal to reach a suitable port they would need to construct the world's longest overland conveyer system, the cost of which Old Dynamite said the company was grossly underestimating.

Whilst Old Dynamite's words could not be taken as facts, they did help explain why the market may believe this company to be fully valued. Also, the earlier talk about a takeover could have already put a bid premium into the stock's price, diminishing its scope for further appreciation.

The coal and the coal mining business was a more complex industry than I had envisioned. It wasn't necessarily the case that finding big coal deposits was the problem, a myriad of other factors all had to be fulfilled for a mine to be viable. I was now beginning to understand why most mining projects didn't get developed. With the market signalling ambivalence towards Churchill's stock it was time to hit the sell button. I had no desire to get caught up in the tangles of another small cap exploration company. I was looking for the line of least resistance to profits and Churchill Mining wasn't it.

A short time after selling out, the share price resumed its slide and soon it was 30% below its peak, then 40%, before finally collapsing and sliding a further 30% in one day. I clicked on the news icon that had appeared next to the stock's price to see what had triggered the latest plunge. Was the news going to be that the company had revised upwards its costings for developing the project? Or could it be that finance wasn't available to develop the project because of its poor location and low quality coal? In fact it was none of these things. Allegations had been made that Churchill had carried out mining activities illegally, consequently several of Churchill's key mining licences had been revoked. The company hadn't made the full extent of its problems with Indonesian officials known to the market immediately, but some news may have leaked out. By watching the market closely, I had successfully detected that something was wrong and had managed to exit the market prior to the official news release.

The stock lost more of its value as the legal wrangling between Churchill and the Indonesian authorities dragged on. Churchill was ultimately exonerated, with many people speculating that the motivation behind the revocation of the licences was that Indonesian officials were trying to extract bribes from Churchill. Churchill has filed for damages that are nearly 30 times the stock's current market value. But in a re-run of earlier events the market is being highly sceptical of Churchill's attempts at self-valuation, with the stock price remaining a fraction of Churchill's estimate of its Net Present Value and the amount of damages it believes it suffered. It does, after all, seem that Old Dynamite's valuation of the project is the one that the market believes to have the greatest validity.

21.1 Learning from Experience

Trading experience helps to develop a trader's sense of the optimal ways to trade developments in the economy or changes in the market. Inevitably when trading we encounter new experiences and have to venture into areas of the market which we are unfamiliar. This is because markets which enjoy strong growth develop rapidly. Eventually they become dogged by overcapacity causing profitability to decline and the companies which once had bright prospects struggle to survive. Money then moves to invest in other sectors of the economy causing demand to rise and new uptrends to form. This causes traders to learn about new sectors of the market.

Despite having to periodically rotate between sectors and learn new skills many of the skills that were acquired trading other sectors are transferrable and can be used to trade stocks regardless of what sector the stock is in. This is one of the major advantages of trend-following.

Fig 25. *Churchill Mining: The Story in a Chart*

1. The stock hits a low during the recession in 2008-2009. Numerous companies snap up shares in the company at depressed valuations. The economy recovers and Churchill shares soar, rising over 600% in 18 months.

2. The stake building by other companies ceases and the share price stalls despite the coal mining sector being one of the most in demand sectors. Good news is issued by the company yet the stock doesn't rise, raising suspicions about the health of the company, triggering the sale of my holding.

3. The share price begins to collapse on very heavy trading volume giving a strong indication that all is not well. On the announcement that the mining licence has been revoked the stock gaps lower on very heavy trading volume giving another warning signal to exit. The stock languishes and doesn't recover.

Lessons Learned

Firstly, businesses are far more complex than is often thought by the observer. I naively believed that coal exploration and mining was a relatively simple business, especially once the resource had been located, yet there are a myriad of factors that mean finding coal is only one of many challenges faced by exploration companies. It took my experience with Churchill as well as owning shares in several other businesses with new products or new projects to realise that new business ventures have a disconcertingly low rate of success, and that the chances of success for new businesses is often grossly overestimated by the market. I now avoid investing in all businesses which are reliant on a new product that is in its formative stages. This is at least partially due to the complexity of modern society, with a broad array of legal and economic hurdles that a new product must cross. The development costs and the marketability of new products are also particularly difficult to determine. My personal experience has lead me to concluded that investment in a company which is dependent on new or bespoke products is only warranted once substantial sales have been reached.

Secondly, the expression 'garbage in, garbage out' is applicable to many calculations and ratios used for investment purposes. If optimistic forecasts are inputted into a calculation then the outcome will also be optimistic. Never accept valuation assessments on face value, they are all based on subjective assumptions about the future trading prospects of the business.

In Churchill's case production of hundreds of millions of tonnes of coal was expected. Therefore, an increase of a few dollars in the estimated selling price of each tonne meant a huge increase in the forecast profitability of Churchill's mining project, thus dramatically increasing the value of the company, since the value of a company is derived from its forecast profitability.

Thirdly, don't become wedded to stocks – In this instance I sold the stock without hesitation, but novice investors are often reluctant to sell. Research has found that when people buy stocks, the investment often embodies their hopes and dreams. Professor David Tuckett, an expert on the psychology of investors, concluded that people come to consider their investments as 'fantastic objects'. A new car, holidays, and the opportunity for a better lifestyle all become associated with the investment. When an investor forms an attachment to stocks it becomes difficult to sell because they feel they are selling something that gives them hope about the future. Investors need to be aware of such tendencies and ruthlessly override them

Fourthly, if you own a great stock it will leap higher on good news, running ahead of the market leading the market higher. If a stock isn't acting as expected, be careful, there may be something wrong. Knowing how a stock price should move can be a time consuming skill to acquire. But there is strong evidence this skill can be developed through market watching, although much of what is learnt may be assimilated into the subconscious areas of the brain. It is said that the legendary trader George Soros frequently developed a crippling back pain when he was badly positioned in the market, even though his conscious brain didn't know exactly what was wrong. One of the most telling examples of the important role repetitive behaviour and the subconscious have in decision making and learning comes from the poultry breeding industry where millions of birds need to be separated according to their sex at a very young age. Trainees to this job are given no other instruction but to look at the rear end of the chick and separate males from females. The teacher then tells them yes or no, but provides no rationale for the judgement. It takes many weeks of intensively repeating this process to separate the males from the females. The thing is they can't tell to you how they do it – their subconscious brain can identify the difference between males and females but their conscious brain is unaware of how they know. To this end, repeatedly examining the charts of great stocks, even if you don't own the stock, helps train the brain to develop a strong awareness of how great stocks should perform, and what the chart of a great stock looks like. In this instance 'sensing' Churchill's stock wasn't performing as it should prevented me from incurring losses of over £35,000.

Fifthly, play great defence when you trade. Like any competitive sport the avoidance of losses is critical in being successful. Take the scenario of a starting investment of £1000 and sustaining a 30% loss leaving £700 to invest. A return of nearly 50% is now needed just to get back to par!

Sixth, investment bulletin boards can occasionally be useful, but the vast majority of people who post aren't knowledgeable investors, although occasionally some excellent posts are published.

Seventh, the information contained in a quality investment newsletter led me to invest in the coal mining sector. Whilst I wouldn't describe the information in the newsletter as a 'tip', this case study highlights the problems of following other people's advice. In particular, if the rationale for making an investment is not well understood then knowing when the rationale for owning the stock has changed is difficult, leaving the trader vulnerable. A trader must know the trades he holds and why, only then can informed decisions be made.

Finally, the potential for a stock price to move higher is limited when there is already a broad consensus that a stock may be taken over and the sector is hot, because much of the good news is priced in. In this instance Churchill stock was purchased near to the peak of a boom, and its price had appreciated significantly in anticipation of a takeover.

22. Trading a Crisis

Since hitting a low point in 2009 the market had risen strongly. The share prices of mining companies had shot higher, like projectiles from a cannon. The value of some mining stocks doubled, most at least tripled, and many increased by more. The previous 18 months saw my portfolio soar in value to now be worth just over £1,000,000. With the market trending higher and valuations still inexpensive my trading plan was to buy aggressively if the market signalled it was about to move another leg higher. I knew markets didn't move in straight lines, periods occur within uptrends when the market pulls back, often sharply, losing 7-12% in value. During these corrections many stock prices fall by as much as 20-30%. Buying immediately after a correction offers advantages, since corrections provide a gauge as to where the buyers will enter the market to abate its fall. They are like a plumb line, dropped into the depths of the market, showing where buying interest is strong. I intended to play the market by waiting for a pullback. Then, when the market had found support and was climbing higher, to significantly increase my exposure to mining stocks as they broke out.

The awaited correction occurred. Although corrections occur without conscious direction the falling market serves the purpose of scaring weak shareholders into selling, clearing the market. Once the process is complete the market can rally upwards to new highs without encountering significant selling pressure. Holding stock whilst the market corrects is never easy, by their nature these periodic sell-offs are uncomfortable. Negative news stories swirl and tumbling prices pressure the trader's hand. Many consecutive days have to be endured when the ground seems to open up, and prices skid scarily lower. Then the market rallies higher, hopes build that the correction is over, only for the market to crash lower, destroying the trader's resilience via the repeated alternation between rallies higher, offering hope, and sharp falls, bringing pain. The correction process can involve the market doing this for up to 12 weeks.

Enduring this correction was to be unusually gruelling, I was holding trades with a value of over £1 million, an experience that was previously foreign and I anticipated that the pressure from the selloff would make this a tough experience. The preparation for the forthcoming challenge could only consist of revising how uncomfortable the price action during a correction would be, but nothing more could be done. Although I expected that this fall would only be a correction and not the start of major fall in the market it was sensible to prepare for the worst, so I had a stop loss point marked on the price chart, with a weekly close below the 200 day moving average on the FTSE 100 triggering my exit.

As the market tumbled I tried to focus through the turbulence, thinking of the day when it would pass, and the market moved higher once again. But this correction seemed particularly severe, however I recalled that the current event always feels worse than those of the past, for, if it was familiar, then the panic it causes would be insufficient to trigger the necessary selling to clear the market. For all my expectations that this would be another standard pullback, it wasn't to be. The selling pressure didn't relent. After a sharp plunge the stop loss level was triggered. I'd lost over £200,000.

The reason for the sudden drop in the market was that over the past decade Greece had accumulated a huge amount of debt, and the market doubted it could be repaid. I knew of Greece's troubles, but the past two years had seen both Iceland and Dubai experience similar debt crises, causing the market only moderate turbulence. On these previous occasions the market digested the news and moved higher. When Greece got into difficulties I didn't see why global markets should be more troubled, since Greece's economy was small, only the size of Washington D.C's, so its problems weren't an obvious reason to derail Europe's $18 trillion economy, and yet it did, with the economic contagion spreading through Europe's economies like a virulent flu.

Over the next 12 months the markets gyrated wildly as traders grappled to assess the severity of the situation. The IMF, ECB and Europe's politicians proposed various solutions. Sometimes a series of optimistic statements that the problems would be resolved took the market higher by more than 10% in only a few days. But for trend followers this was problematic since it often gave a signal to buy, only for the market to dive lower again as tougher talk resurfaced. False signals to enter new trades occurred repeatedly, each one biting a chunk of wealth from the trading account.

On account of the number of false signals generated, I considered jettisoning the trend-following methodology. But what if the next buy signal was ignored, only for it to be accurate and the market to charge higher without pause, leaving me deprived of a foothold in the market? Continuing with my existing methodology, but with a reduced stake seemed the best option. But trading continued to be fruitless. Share prices gyrated wildly and the tremendous volatility caused the price to cut through chart patterns like a knife, rendering technical analysis useless.

European politicians and officials proposed more financial packages to stem the crisis, each time offering reassurances that this one would save the Eurozone, but they proved to be only a Band-Aid that covered, but didn't heal, the wounds at the heart of Europe's financial system. The crisis grew more intense and many economies suffered deeply. The worsening economy triggered harder rhetoric from the politicians and the old divisions within Europe rose to the surface. The Germans tried to conceal that they now dominated Europe, but many other European countries were in their debt and the dream of a Europe of equal states living in harmony was eroding. To ensure repayment creditor nations such as Germany sought to dictate the governance of other European states that they regarded as dysfunctional. There seemed little common ground between debtors and creditors. The fault lines were exposed, dissolution of the European Union seemed imminent.

The rolling tides of panic and fear swirling in the market rendered every type of analysis I tried ineffective. A new approach was needed and I set to learning about the economics and politics that lay at the heart of Europe's current crisis. I avidly read The Economist and The Financial Times. After several months study Europe's problems seemed clearer. I concluded that Europe had become unbalanced with heavy debt loads in some countries, and with no ways of repayment the union would fall apart unless agreement could be reached on sharing the burden. But this solution was unacceptable to many creditor nations.

The newspapers and journals reported conflict between Europe's politicians was growing more intense. Business confidence across Europe fell and recession looked near. Investor faith in Europe's financial system was depleted to such a low level that Europe's mountain of debt looked close to toppling. Media pundits predicted the problems were now insoluble. A forthcoming political summit to resolve the deepening crisis looked certain to fail and the European Union would dissolve. That week The Economist ran over 10 stories speculating about the impeding breakup of Europe; not one story proposed Europe could heal its wounds. Respected columnists in the Financial Times also argued that the fragmentation of Europe was imminent and European stock markets dived, losing a whopping 20% in just a few weeks. The media opinion seemed logical, so my trading reflected this hypothesis.

As Europe teetered on collapse markets stopped falling. It was reported that several highly successful hedge fund managers were aggressively investing money in the distressed European nations, but to my frustration I couldn't discover their reasoning. The politicians from creditor nations continued to demand tough economic measures be implemented to ensure repayment. The southern nations issued equally robust responses. The political rhetoric lent no support to the idea that the major European summit which had been arranged to resolve Europe's economic crisis could be a success, yet the volatility dissipated from the market. It became calm, and then markets climbed higher. As the critical European summit drew close robust words from politicians bounced off the market, unable to knock it back down. Then, against media consensus, the summit was announced a success, with a comprehensive agreement reached between the creditor and debtor nations. The politicians shock hands like old friends and markets rose like a firework. The elite traders who had invested at the climax of the crisis enjoyed huge rewards. I belatedly joined the party and earned a small sum, but without a better understanding of the situation I refrained from significant involvement.

How had the elite traders foretold the outcome of the summit? Why had others, including me, been so wrong-footed? In order to gain some trading insights I needed to understand the rational for the actions of the elite traders.

Finding Out

The elite traders held a different perspective on the likely outcome to events than that published in the media, and they confidently disregarded the tough political rhetoric that made compromise seem impossible. They understood Europe not by what people said, or what the media published, but by understanding the interests of each group involved in the crisis. There were three important groups who influenced the market. The politicians of the creditor nations, led by Germany; the politicians of the debtor nations, led by Spain and Italy; and the media who transmitted the message and influenced public opinion. The politicians of both the creditor and debtor nations had common goals, they were keen to be seen defending national interests on the international stage, issuing tough rhetoric to a public that wanted their leaders to concede nothing in the latest European battle. But the politicians were controlled by another powerful motive, they are the puppets of powerful economic interests within their nations. They needed to balance the rhetoric with demands from the powerful interest groups back home. Germany, the strongest country in Europe, benefited tremendously from the development of the European Union. The powerful exporting companies of Germany, such as Volkswagen and BMW, desperately needed access to the markets of other European nations to sell their goods. If countries left the Eurozone they might block German imports, leaving piles of unsold stock and huge losses. Germany also benefited from the weak euro which resulted from sharing a currency with weaker economies. If the weaker countries left the Euro then the currency would strengthen, making German exports significantly more expensive. German banks had also made loans totalling many hundreds of billions of Euros to the Southern European states which might not be repaid if the Eurozone fragmented and debtor nations collapsed. Germany, despite its tough rhetoric desperately needed to hold Europe together.

On the other side of the divide were the debtor nations of Greece, Spain, Italy, Ireland and Portugal. Their leaders needed to demonstrate that their nations would not be bullied. They understood Germany's weaknesses, so were confident to talk tough. Still, leaving the euro would mean economic hardship for them, remaining in the Eurozone was desirable. After months of endless research it had proved simple to understand the mechanics of the Eurozone providing that, as a trader, I focused on the right thing. In this instance predicting the outcome was simply down to comprehending the interests of each nation within the Eurozone.

Whilst Europe's economic crisis was real, many of the speeches made by politicians were media theatre performed for their electorate, resembling an international punch and Judy show. The media profited from the great material that the crisis gave, creating thrilling stories of imminent doom that sold newspapers and hooked viewers. For the politicians, they maximised the opportunity to be statesmen on the international stage, using the opportunity to grow their approval ratings as they battled for their national interests. The elite hedge funds who really understood what was happening made piles of money, cashing in on the panic created by the political rhetoric. Unlike them, I paid another large tuition fee to learn how the world really worked!

Lessons Learned

Firstly, during an international economic crisis the interests of each nation must be understood, only then can outcomes be predicted.

Secondly, the media is not a true reflection of reality - market fluctuations and panics generate significant media noise, much of which doesn't reflect reality. Seek to identify the signal from the noise.

Thirdly, technical analysis and trend following are very useful in most markets, but are of less use when markets are highly volatile.

Finally, during a crisis it is only on the precipice of financial chaos that tough agreements and reforms will be made because crisis resolution entails policies that would normally face public opposition, such as bailing out failed banks, or indebted governments. It is only in moments of financial chaos when the entire financial system is in jeopardy that such policies can be implemented, otherwise public opposition is too strong.

23. This Time it's Different

'You can learn a lot just by watching' Yoga Berra

In this chapter we increase our understanding of markets by exploring the situation in China to illustrate economics and how it can influence trading decisions. When I was trading the boom in metals prices China presented a major dilemma. The continuation of strong economic growth in China was critical because mining stocks filled my trading account and the stocks I was betting on so heavily were dependent on booming demand growth from the Chinese economy. But there was a problem. The uptrend in mining stocks had stalled over a year ago and despite strong economic growth and most traders being highly optimistic about the sector the price performance told a different story. Some traders no longer believed the outlook for mining stocks to be good. But why not?

The investors who were selling their mining stocks and moving out of the sector weren't the guys who listened to the stock brokers and market analysts speaking on CNBC or Bloomberg who were continuing to express the well-known consensus that booming demand from China would continue for decades, consequently there must be other investors holding an alternative analysis. What this viewpoint was, and why they believed the market consensus incorrect became a nagging question that I wanted answered, for it had to be dangerous to own stocks and only know positive reasons for owning them. I would have to analyse the supply and demand situation for the metals market and try to decide the outlook for the metals that the mining sector supplied. I questioned my ability to analyse the metals market, it wasn't my forte, but the continued slippage in mining stock valuations and the establishment of new downtrends in some mining stocks signalled a failing market. I would have to give it my best shot.

23.1 Analysing China

I did an outline assessment of metal consumption in each country and found China gobbling up an astounding 10 times more metal than countries such as India, which also had a very large population and rapidly growing economy. Chinese demand had exploded during the previous decade and was responsible for most of the change in global demand. As a first step I researched why China consumed disproportionately more than similar nations, and why demand had grown so quickly. If I understood what had driven Chinese demand growth I might understand if the drivers were slowing, or more worryingly, about to go into reverse.

I learned that much of the Chinese economy was planned and coordinated by powerful government bureaucracies who developed plans years in advance specifying how much the economy should grow and where resources should be allocated to achieve the government's economic plan. This managed approach to economic development was acknowledged as being vital in enabling the Chinese to achieve tremendous economic success. But the more I learned about the Chinese economic miracle, the less was my belief that it could continue.

The fact that the government planned economic growth, deciding which sectors would receive investment, had strong similarities to the Russian and Eastern European economies when they were under communist rule. These economies had collapsed because the government was unable to manage the economy. It proved too difficult a task because economies are too intricate for bureaucratic planning, demonstrating that large scale economic planning by governments shouldn't be done. I reasoned that the outcome of government planning on the development of the world's second largest economy had to have resulted in wastefulness and the unprecedented misallocation of resources. China's other source of probable weakness was that over the past 30 years they had experienced the largest economic boom in history. The theory of the boom bust cycle (discussed in the next chapter) required the assumption that Chinas economic miracle would, somewhere along the way, encounter a nasty bust phase, when all of the excesses accumulated during the boom suddenly unwind.

The culprit behind the illusion of long periods of economic prosperity during booms is often rapid credit growth, since credit fuels economic activity. It inflates economic performance, driving up property prices, company profits, stock prices and wages. Often the government presiding over the boom foolishly believes that it is actually their good economic policies that have caused the economic miracle, but when the supply of easy credit runs dry the boom degenerates into a vicious bust. It becomes apparent that the proceeding years have been an economic illusion of prosperity created by credit fuelled spending. Politicians often run their nations with all the financial acumen of an 18-year-old with a platinum credit card, and once the credit card hits its limit the party abruptly ends. Not only must the country then live within its limits, the debt must be repaid. This is the bust phase.

To ascertain how proximal China was to the bust phase some sources advised examining the default rate on loans, as this often signalled oncoming problems. The official Chinese statistics said that the rate of non-performing loans in China over the past decade was one quarter of the global average. This struck me as unbelievable, a country with almost no bad loans after decades of booming growth defied almost all that economic history could teach. I had heard rumours that Chinese economic statistics were manipulated, but this statistic stunk like old roadkill.

Further investigation provided additional reasons to believe that the Chinese growth story was rotten, for there was good reason to falsify the nation's economic performance. China's leaders were not democratically elected, instead they held onto power via an implicit promise to achieve national prosperity. Fulfilling this mandate meant retaining power, but what would happen if the economy floundered? With no alternative political party to take power a sudden power struggle could occur, and with China having a long history of civil war, its escalation to violent conflict could not be ruled out. Did this eventuality scare the Chinese leadership so much that they were pumping the economy full of credit and manipulating the economy to maintain a charade of prosperity?

Finding the Truth

I discovered this may be true. In 2008, when the 'credit crunch' pushed the economies of Europe and the United States into recession Chinese exporters suffered greatly. To offset lost growth the Chinese ordered their banks to lend huge amounts of money for new construction projects. The scale and rapidity of China's credit boom which occurred as a result of these policies made anything ever seen in western economies look tame, therefore the accumulated problems within the economy could be huge. But credit fuelled booms are dangerous. The credit crunch recession that had hit Europe and the United States hard in 2008 exemplified the dangers of credit driven economic booms.

The cycle of boom and bust in Europe and America that caused the great recession of 2008 inspired two Harvard economists, Reinhart and Rogoff, to write a bestselling book called *This Time is Different, Eight Centuries of Financial Folly.*[4] The book details how, despite centuries of repeating credit cycles fuelling booms and busts, investors never grasp that credit is a serious danger to economic stability. Reinhart and Rogoff eloquently describe the tranquillity before an economic crash

> "Highly indebted governments, banks or corporations can seem to be merrily rolling along for an extended period, when bang! – confidence collapses, lenders disappear, and crisis hits."

The lesson from the book is don't expect to hear loud dissenting voices about how dangerous a credit fuelled boom is when it is occurring. When everything is OK people don't identify danger, instead they believe that this time it will be different.

Even so soon after the credit crunch when Reinhart and Rogoff's book had triggered widespread head nodding and finger pointing about the dangers of debt, investors were unable to control their excitement about China's economic boom. Investors, stock brokers and economic advisers all concluded that this time it was different. They would then recite a list of reasons why Chinese economic growth was an unstoppable juggernaut which could defy the boom bust cycle.

Even though the hot Chinese economy had inflicted concussive amnesia on the financial community, the continuing soggy share price performance of the mining sector and other China related investments indicated that a select group of investors recalled the lessons of history and saw the danger. One prominent hedge fund manager who hadn't drunk the Chinese Kool-Aid spoke out about China. He had made his name and his billion-dollar fortune trading that the market consensus was wrong and his opinion, and the evidence he presented, proved decisive in answering my conundrum as to whether to own mining stocks.

The hedge fund manager's name was Jim Chanos and on a T.V. show he argued that in his opinion the Chinese economy was experiencing an unsustainable boom, fuelled by rapid growth in credit. China, he said, had to make substantial changes or risk economic collapse. Chanos didn't fit the stereotypical hedge fund manager, he didn't dress as sharply as the Wall Street types or speak their hyper fast jargon. Instead he spoke in slow thoughtful sentences, with every aspect of his opinion supported by facts. He had named his hedge fund 'Kynikos' which was Greek for 'cynic'. His cynical viewpoint had proved instrumental in his success. Whenever Wall Street believed it knew an investment that would provide a stream of endless wealth Chanos would carefully be examining the other side of the trade, looking for the hole in the boat that could eventually cause its capsizing.

Chanos talks China

On the T.V show Chanos was pitched alone against a cast of smartly dressed Wall Street types, all wildly optimistic about China. One of the primary thrusts of their attacks against Chanos' negative opinion stemmed from the fact that he couldn't understand China because he hadn't visited the country for many years and hadn't seen at first-hand the amazing growth that was occurring. Chanos said that observation could be misleading, relying on observation would lead us to believe that the world was flat, instead he emphasised statistical analysis. He stated that in 2012 China planned to build a colossal 10 billion square meters of real estate vs 5.7 billion in 2009 and on the drawing board had another 5.5. Cubic ft. of office space for every man woman and child in China. He pointed out that mining companies had ramped up spending on expanding production to provide the copper, iron, nickel and other raw materials used primarily in construction, and their annual budget for finding more metal ore had increased 1000% over the past 10 years ago, resulting in an avalanche of new supply now hitting the market.

He also drew attention to a statement made by the Chinese Premier 5 years earlier when he stated 'there are structural problems in China's economy which cause unsteady, unbalanced, uncoordinated and unsustainable development'. Premier Wen was intimating that China had experienced a huge construction boom which had destabilised the economy. Following Wen's speech, debt growth had accelerated, and the Chinese economy had become even more unbalanced and unstable as construction continued booming, with spending on new building growing at between 20-50% per year. Chanos aegued that the rates of investment in China suggested that the size and scale of bad investments was huge. Within a few minutes of appearing on television Chanos had blitzed the Wall Street 'experts' into silence. He had shown that their analysis was based upon little more than accepting the economic numbers published by the Chinese government, being wowed by China's expanding skyline of shiny new buildings, and then extrapolating the past rates of economic growth into the future. Expertly, Chanos had examined China's economic engine and seen the monkey wrenches in it. He knew that it was only a matter of time before the engine spluttered and failed.

Chanos went on to highlight instances of wastefulness within China's economy. One example was the city of Ordos. Built under a government plan to accommodate over 1 million people, the city was a tourist attraction. Not because of anything remarkable, but because it was the least inhabited city in the world. Rows of skyscrapers line up, but at night most remain unlit. Despite this, new construction was blindly continuing in line with the government's growth plan. My own research found that in China's smaller cities five years after construction 20% of all buildings remain uninhabited and roads, rails and factories are also overbuilt and underused, with excess capacity easily observable. Hedge fund employees had been visiting China, counting the number of unoccupied buildings. They also travelled railways and roads to assess underutilisation. The managers of these hedge funds understood that Chinese economic data was unreliable and unconventional methods had to be used to assess the health of the economy.

Scratching behind China's starry rates of economic growth revealed a dysfunctional economy that was becoming increasingly unstable. The longer the boom persisted the greater the problems would become. I became certain that the Chinese economy would ultimately face a moment of truth when its weakness would be revealed. Economic weakness would bring additional concerns about the governance of the world's second most powerful economy, potentially triggering enormous social and economic upheaval as the people of China strove not just for a better economy, but also for a better government. With a history of large scale conflict within its borders, the fabric that held China together could once again become strained.

23.2 Lessons Learned

Firstly, technical analysis of mining companies that depend on Chinese demand provided the first signal that all was not well with the Chinese economy. Investigating why the market failed to do what was expected once again yielded insights into the true state of affairs.

Secondly, China's boom bust cycle is an excellent example for observant traders to learn and understand future boom bust cycles. The boom bust cycle repeats throughout history and traders who have observed one boom and bust cycle have a road map to trade future cycles. Trend-following traders are ideally suited to identify and trade these highly profitable situations.

Thirdly, during economic booms there is the media narrative of what is happening, and then there is reality. A large gulf exists between the media perspective and the truth.

Fourthly, the boom bust cycle is a powerful lens for traders. It facilitates seeing why markets form large trends, but also that booms are unsustainable. When the bust phase occurs all of the fault lines that have grown underneath the boom are exposed along with the falseness of the media narrative which accompanied the boom.

Fifthly, whilst each boom bust cycle has its own peculiarities, they also have common characteristics - the next passage was written after boom and bust in America in the 1920's

"Even in such a time of madness as the late twenties, a great many men on Wall Street remained quite sane. But they also remained very quiet. The sense of responsibility in the financial community for the community as a whole is not small. It is nearly nil. Perhaps this is inherent. In a community where the primary concern is making money, one of the necessary rules is to live and let live. To speak out against madness maybe to ruin those who succumb to it. So the wise on Wall Street are nearly always silent. The fools thus have the field to themselves". John K Galbraith.

The wise were almost always silent in booms then, and they remain almost unheard now, except for the occasional dissenting voice such as Chanos' outspoken opinion. The lesson is that markets that undergo a boom develop an aura of invincibility that isn't questioned until after the boom has passed and the bust phase has become so ugly that its occurrence cannot be denied. Traders should ignore the media narrative that accompanies the boom, it is a fallacy that is created to justify the prices that define a boom. Focus on the trend and on identifying the faults in the rationale that underpins the boom. When the trend ends these faults will be exposed like crumbling brickwork behind plaster.

Finally, trade in the direction of the trend, but beware of stalling trends. This indicates the market is balanced and could move sharply.

Trading boom bust cycles doesn't require expertise in economics or politics to succeed. A curious and enquiring mind and good skills with an internet search engine can enable a trader to see beyond the market consensus to find the truth.

Throughout this book so far we have navigated a whole series of boom and busts ranging from the internet boom, to the housing market boom, as well as the mining and commodities boom and the Chinese economic boom. All of these events produced highly tradable trends, which provided outstanding profit opportunities. To not recognise boom bust cycles as outstanding trading opportunities would therefore be foolish. In fact, can it not be said that the best trend-following opportunities always relate to those that accompany the boom bust cycle? I believe so.

Cognisant of the importance of the boom bust cycle, we now build on our understanding of booms and busts, and how to trade them, encapsulating the boom bust cycle into a simple model.

24. The Boom Bust Model

When encountering complex situations it is wise to create a model that facilitates understanding. Condensing a large number of complex factors into only the essential frees the mind of complexity, enabling a clearer vision. The boom bust model is one such tool which enables the various stages of the boom bust cycle to be represented in a simple 4 stage diagram, enabling a trader to know his location on the cycle

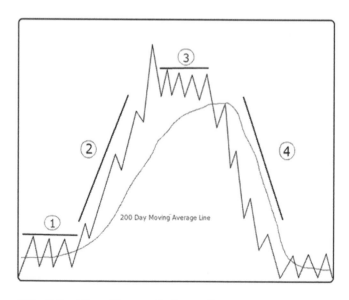

Fig 26. *How Prices Behave During a Boom Bust Cycle*

(1) During phase 1 the price is trapped in a trading range below the line marked 1. In this phase there is minimal interest in the sector from investors and the media. Major investors, such as pension funds often own a minimal number of shares in the sector due to its previous underperformance, or perceived lack of good prospects.

(2) The market breaks out from its trading range below line 1, giving a buy signal to trend followers. It enters phase 2. The amount of commentary in the media remains minimal and 'experts' express cynicism that the price rise will be sustained, but prices continue to rise and the sector becomes the best performing sector in the market. Many investors, such as pension funds, now need to buy the shares because they don't own enough shares in the sector. They do this because if the shares continue to outperform their fund will lag behind that of competing funds who own more shares in the hot sector. This additional buying causes share prices to rise further.   Comment in the media about the sector increases, along with investor interest.   Stock brokerages sense the opportunity to generate additional commissions from share trading by encouraging investors to sell some of their existing shares and buy more shares in the new hot sector, which they market as having fantastic opportunities for growth and profits, issuing analysis in the form of highly optimistic brokerage research notes, fanning the flames of interest now burning brightly around the sector. Growing awareness of the sector and its strong price performance triggers increased media coverage, perpetuating investor interest. The readership of the mainstream media doesn't want a longwinded justification for all of the reasons why the shares in the sector are performing strongly, so a simplified media narrative develops to justify the previous share price rises and why the outlook for the sector is bright. As share prices continue to increase rapidly confidence grows, encouraging investors to buy more shares as the market roars higher. The market develops a herd mentality.

(3) After many years of booming prices the media narrative becomes accepted wisdom. This is repeated without question. The boom is widely known about and much is written about the exciting opportunities. The few who question it are treated with suspicion. Whilst confidence in the sector is now at its highest, the outlook for the companies in the sector is weakening. That's because the abundance of new money flooding into the sector in previous years has triggered entrepreneurs to start new companies which increases competition, yet this is unmentioned in the broker reports and the media. Investors who conduct deeper market analysis see that the outlook is dimming and that profits are threatened. The market is in its twilight period. They sell, checking further price rises in the value of the sector. High prices are no longer justified, yet the price remains supported on a high ledge by virgin investors, drawn to the sector by past price gains and the positive media commentary.

(4) Shares in the sector are now widely owned. New buying interest is insufficient to maintain prices within phase 3. The market price breaks lower and a new downtrend commences. Technical analysis gives a strong sell signal when support for the market snaps. Uninformed investors view lower prices as a bargain and buy, causing the price to periodically bounce sharply higher. The media continue to be positive about the market. However, the developing downtrend nullifies the validity of the existing optimistic media narrative, which must now be changed to a negative narration to explain the falling market. Share prices crumble as more sellers dash to escape the falling market.

Company chief executives in the formerly hot sector cite reasons why their companies are failing to meet profit targets. In the early stages of phase 4 many of them express confidence that the current setbacks are a temporary blip, causing the market to rally sharply, but each time the rally fails. Stockbrokerages and analysts change their recommendations to reflect the falling prices, pushing the market lower. They now sense the opportunity to generate revenues by getting clients to sell out of the once hot sector and 'rotate money into a safe sector'. Their clients, feeling pain from mounting losses, gladly comply, pressuring the share prices even lower – but growing the profits and revenues of the broker! The media changes tack to sensationalise and rationalise the bust phase, using such words as 'crash' and 'collapse' helping trigger the capitulation of the remaining shareholders. As phase 4 develops the prominence of the faults that have been undermining the sector grow. Underfunded companies go bankrupt; others struggle as banks become cautious about lending more money to the ailing sector. By the later stages of phase 4 there is widespread awareness of the crash and the reasons why the market is weak.

Now look at a chart of a stock that went through the commodities boom bust cycle

Fig 27. *Chart Showing the Four Stages of the Boom Bust Cycle*

During phase 1 the share price rise is slow and gains are not eye-catching. In phase 2 the market breaks out and the rate of ascent rises. At phase 3 the market commentary remains positive yet the share price stalls. 4 marks the start of the downtrend which is as yet incomplete since the trend is still lower and has yet to reverse.

The boom phase of the boom bust cycle happens at a slower pace than the bust phase. Scientists have identified the reasons to explain why this is. This is the subject of the next section.

25. Market Crashes

25.1 Natural Phenomena and Markets

In similarity to financial markets, an ecosystem has millions of individual organisms which are diverse and autonomous, but they also share an interdependency. Like bricks in a wall, the absence or weakness of some can cause the entire structure to collapse. Ecosystems often undergo spontaneous changes, such as when a forest fire or avalanche occurs. In these instances, they transition from a seemingly stable condition into a state of chaos. Understanding how and why natural phenomena undergo these transitions helps us understand markets, and especially why they are prone to crash.

25.2 The Scientific Model

Scientists constructed a simple model to simulate how complex systems such as ecosystems and financial markets undergo sudden changes, and why. It consisted of forming a pile of sand by dropping individual grains of sand, a single grain at a time, onto a pile and observing the stability of the sand pile as it grew. They were seeking to identify when the pile would collapse. Unfortunately, the scientists concluded that there was no way of predicting its exact timing, although they learned that the risk of collapse increased as the sand pile grew. But the big breakthrough came when researchers substituted the tedious task of forming real sand piles with a computer simulation. The simulation enabled the speedy replication of the sand pile experiment, and importantly, a much greater analysis of the time surrounding collapse. Scientists could accurately measure the steepness in each of the areas of the pile, as well as studying the condition of the entire pile before collapse.

The computer simulation colour coded the areas of the pile according to their steepness. Relatively flat areas were colour coded green, and the steeper areas coloured red. The results from the simulation showed that when the pile was mostly green the chance of collapse was remote, with only minor dislocations occurring. As sand grains were added and the pile grew higher the red areas on the pile increased, and the result of each additional grain became less predictable. Each added grain could cause a minor dislocation, or it could cause the entire pile to collapse. They found that collapse was much more likely as the number of red areas increased, leading them to conclude that each area of red was a point of instability. As the points of instability increased so did the likelihood of collapse. In the moments prior to collapse, when the sand pile is riddled with points of instability it is said to be in a critical state because the sand pile could, at any moment, collapse. Similar phenomena are observed in other natural occurrences such as forest fires. Prior to the occurrence of the fire highly flammable material has accumulated to such a level that the forest is in a critical state. The longer time that passes without the occurrence of a fire the more critical the risk of fire becomes. When the fire occurs the forest goes through a major transition, the instability is removed, and the forest returns to a more stable state. It is now unlikely to experience another similar event for a long time. A further analogy is that of snow balanced high up on a mountain. As more and more snowflakes fall the amount of snow on the mountain increases, becoming more and more unstable and the more the snow accumulates the greater the points of instability and the greater the risk of avalanche.

25.3 Critical States and the Stock Market

In resemblance to the action of how forming a sand pile results in the occurrence of a critical state, it is known that trading activity can form a critical state in financial markets, explaining why markets periodically crash. If we consider each trade placed in the market to be represented by a sand grain, and the sand pile to be the market, we can see the similarity that the sand pile represents a model of the market - as more and more traders take positions and confidence grows that the market will move in a particular direction the market becomes increasingly unstable. This is confirmed by examining the history of the stock market crashes that occurred in 1929, 1987 and 2001. Each crash happened after very large moves higher in the stock market, and, at the peak of each market, traders exhibited an extreme level of confidence and commitment to the market.

25.4 Uncertainty and Decision Making

When trading in a market the value of an investment is only worth what another trader is willing to pay. A cacophony of factors influence the market price, therefore the value of all investments that are freely traded on markets is uncertain. Scientist have recognised that when uncertainty is present decision making undergoes important changes. They ascertained that human decisions are not bounded by the cold, hard reason scientists had formerly thought was the basis of our actions. Non-obvious reasons have been identified as influencing the decisions we make. Scientists refer to these influences as *biases,* because they bias the decisions we make. There are many different biases that influence our opinions and therefore when people trade in markets these factors influence the market price.

Groupthink Bias

The investment community can be regarded as a large group of people dispersed throughout the world. They are interconnected by means of communication, such as the media, stockbrokers, blogs, investor conferences, email, phone conversations and personal contact. The opinions of others in the group, especially respected sources, influences our decision making. One of the most insightful psychological experiments to understand the extent of this influence was conducted in 1951 by Solomon Asch. He proved that our decisions are heavily influenced by wishing to conform to other group members, even to the extent that the opinion of the group outweighs individual beliefs. He demonstrated this in a simple experiment.

Box 1   Box 2

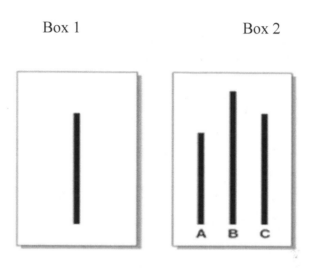

The card in box 1 shows a reference line, the card in box 2 shows the three comparison lines. Asch's experiments consisted of a simple question. Is the line in box 1 most similar to the line A, B or C in box 2?

The participants in the experiment were formed into groups except that in each group all of the other people were actors. The actors in the group had all been instructed to give the same wrong answer. The non-actor was unaware of this. The actors individually stated their answer out loud first in the presence of the other group members. They were instructed to say the incorrect answer, line A. The participant was then instructed to give their answer, so that the effect of hearing the obviously incorrect answer from each of the other members of the group (the actors) could be assessed. How would the answer given be affected by the same incorrect answer been given by the rest of the group? The results were astonishing. The vast majority of people were overwhelmingly influenced by the answers of others, with over 75% of people giving the same wrong answer as the actors had been instructed to give, as opposed to a 1%

error rate when the test was taken in isolation. The conclusion of the experiment provided hard evidence that the vast majority of people were prejudiced by the decisions of others. But the experiment revealed another strange phenomenon about the influence group pressure can exert on decision making.

During interviews conducted after the experiment, participants were questioned about the answers they had given. Whilst most participants were aware that they were giving the incorrect answer and knew that they had yielded to group pressure, the interviewers found significant numbers of people actually believed the answer given by the group of actors was correct and they believed that the answer they gave was also correct. The scientists concluded that these participants had experienced perception shift as a result of their biological need to conform to the group, demonstrating that the subconscious brain can alter our perceptions to facilitate conformity with the group.

This experiment, and the conclusions of subsequent experiments, demonstrated that groups have a powerful ability to influence our decision making. Herding and groupthink influence markets, forming trends in asset prices as people's thoughts converge on what they should buy, creating cycles of boom busts. Research has found that as markets rise the amount of positive opinions on the markets increase and that confidence is at its highest level when the market peaks. This is the time when stock brokerages have the highest number of buy recommendations and the media publishes its most upbeat stories about the prospects for the market. It is this type of behaviour that causes markets to become unbalanced and to enter a critical state where it is prone to collapse.

Subsequent to Asch's experiment researchers discovered many other biases that influence human behaviour. The ones which are most pertinent to investing are:-

Anchoring bias – Researchers discovered that mentioning a random number to people and then asking them a question with a numerical answer influences the answer they give. To demonstrate this, scientists randomly selected subjects and asked them to guess how much an unlabelled bottle of champagne cost. But the question had an added twist. When asking about the price of the champagne the researcher mentioned a random number. They found that this number served as an anchor and strongly influenced the valuation given for the bottle of champagne. For example, if the researcher mentioned the number 10, then the answer given was more likely to be closer to £10 than if the number 10 had not been mentioned. In markets this effect can be powerful, it shows how people's opinions about the price of an asset can be influenced by opinions in the media, internet chatter and analyst's reports that propose a value for a stock.

Loss Aversion Bias – Scientific experiments show that people who lose £100 experience greater dissatisfaction and pain than they would experience pleasure and satisfaction from gaining £100. Studies suggest that losses have double the psychological influence of an equivalent gain. Knowing the power of emotional pain inflicted by losses explains why investors feel compelled to sell stocks which have fallen significantly in value. Even if investors believe a stock is cheap, a falling price can inflict powerful feelings of pain and discomfort, pressuring the investor to exit a losing position. Understanding this bias helps explain why stocks which have fallen, even to extremely cheap valuations, often fail to attract buyers, and instead attract more selling. There is a proverb in the stock market that says 'don't catch a falling knife' – meaning don't buy a share that is falling sharply - the risk aversion bias provides rationale for the proverb.

Recent Event Bias – When making decisions the human brain weights recent events more heavily than those that occurred further in the past. From an investment point of view this means that investors are more heavily influenced by the recent market direction and whether they have made gains or losses in a market. This bias contributes to the formation of market trends as investment decisions are influenced by whether existing investment returns are positive or negative. Investors are likely to allocate more capital to markets where the recent return on investment is positive, accentuating an existing market trend.

Myopia Bias – Myopia Bias has a perceptible impact on the daily movements of market prices. The theory of the stock market is that earning per share drives stock price movements, but this is not the case in the very near term. Stock prices have been shown to fluctuate much more than should be the case if investors were rational and were solely focused on the returns on offer, indicating that investor behaviour is marred by short-sightedness.

Hyperbolic Discounting Bias– Traders prefer to invest in markets that offer the opportunity for immediate capital appreciation. This bias provides a rationale as to why investors are drawn to markets that are moving strongly in one direction and provides at least a partial explanation as to why many investors favour assets that are appreciating rapidly, even if valuations are expensive.

Ikea Effect -People are slower to recognise an idea as substandard if they have been involved in its creation. In the investment arena, this bias manifest itself by traders continuing to hold underperforming stocks even in the face of strong evidence that the premise of the trade is no longer valid.

Risk Taking Bias – Research confirms that risk taking increases with the number of positive results attained. From a trading perspective this means that when markets perform strongly traders increase risk, ploughing more money into the market and pushing it yet higher. In doing so they create a positive feedback loop, validating previous trades and raising confidence levels, encouraging yet more investment in the market. The Risk Taking Bias helps to explain why market trends persist and why markets often become overvalued.

Risk Aversion Bias –The risk aversion bias is the counterpart to the risk taking bias. Traders experience increasing risk aversion as losses increase. This bias helps to explain why investors are less inclined to buy when the market falls.

Information Bias – The more information investors have the more confidence they have in their decision making, even if much of that information is irrelevant. Many of the indicators in technical analysis such as momentum indicators, Fibonacci sequences and patterns used in technical analysis tell us little useful information about the direction of the market, yet they are routinely used by traders. The use of such methods is promoted by some stock brokerages to present the idea that the market is predictable with pinpoint accuracy, encouraging traders to believe they hold useful information and encouraging them to take risks.

Confirmation Bias –The tendency to search for, interpret, and focus on information that confirms our preconceptions. When researching trade ideas, we are biased towards giving favourable interpretations to data that supports are existing thoughts, and to find reasons to dismiss information that is not constructive to validating our existing opinion.

Bereavement Bias – Researchers found that it takes on average 18 months for a person to recover from the loss of a loved one. When applied to financial markets it explains why many investors take several years to re-enter a market when they have suffered significant losses. The bias may explain why, after a sustained fall in which many investors suffer large losses, markets can remain at low valuations for a longer period than expected.

The Principal/Agent Bias – Most of the money invested in financial markets is controlled by professional fund managers. Therefore most money has a Principal. This person is the owner or person with overall responsibility for the money. It will also have an Agent. The Agent is the individual fund manager charged with making investment decisions. The Principal assesses the competency of the Agent, ensuring he is capable of discharging the role. This takes the form of periodically reporting the performance of the fund to the Principal. The competency of the fund manager is assessed according to the portfolio's performance in comparison to other funds and the market which the fund is benchmarked against. At face value, this is a rational action. But the Principal undertakes this exercise to determine if he has selected a suitable agent. The agent understands that his performance will be compared to his peers. If an agent's performance lags, deselection as fund manager is a very real possibility. Again, at first glance this seems rational and responsible, but it can have a distorting influence on markets. It encourages fund managers to select a portfolio that will track the market and hug the performance of other funds, and not necessarily to seek investments that they believe offer the best prospects. When reviewing the previous biases we have already seen that investors are biased towards risk aversion when a stock or market has fallen. If a fund manager buys falling stocks which are out of favour, then he differentiates himself from other fund managers. If the fund manager is right, he will outperform his competitors, if he is wrong his fund will underperform and he may be deselected as fund manager. Because the bonus for outperforming is small compared to the benefit of maintaining his employment, it is wise for the manger to focus on avoiding risks and hugging the performance of other fund managers – in short – herding behaviour is rewarded by the way in which fund managers' remuneration is structured.

To illustrate this important point, let's look at the example of the period 1999-2001. In 1999 stocks were trading at record valuations, technology stocks in particular enjoyed exuberant valuations. In the market environment of 1999 it would seem rational for a fund manager to avoid the most overvalued areas and invest in lower valuation stocks. But 1999 saw a further surge in investor interest in technology stocks, causing the technology sector to jump higher. A fund manager who adopted the strategy of avoiding ridiculously priced technology stocks now faces a dilemma, if his performance falls further behind, investors may withdraw capital. The fund manager can alleviate this risk by increasing investment in the technology sector, in doing so he will likely retain his job and the trust of his investors in the fund. If the fund manager fails to invest, he would have been wrong-footed yet again because in the later part of 1999, the inflow of funds from private investors destined for the technology sector surged and propelled the market still higher. The fund manager faces intense pressure to invest. If the market rises further and he's not invested he could be seen as incompetent. Most prudent investors who tried to avoid the overvalued technology sector did, at some point capitulate, fuelling the expansion of the bubble and placing additional pressure on other investors to also make investments. By 2001 the bubble burst and the stock market collapsed. Although the market crashed, those fund managers who lost a similar amount to the average fund manager kept their jobs. Even the very best investors can be wrong footed by booms. The legendary investor Stan Drukenmillar, who is one of the most successful investors alive today suffered large losses following the boom in technology stocks. He invested in the technology bubble early and rode the market's trend higher, exiting when valuations became expensive, earning huge profits. But the boom continued and the pressure to partake in one of the largest booms in history caused him to re-enter the market at its peak and after just a few months the crashing market caused him to accrue losses of $2bn.

Because stocks were so obviously overvalued during the technology boom it provides a classic example to illustrate the mechanics underlying the market. The relationship between the Principle and the Agent results in the vast majority of fund managers not being free from outside influence on how they invest. In reality most fund managers have little choice but to ensure that they follow the market.

The Principal / Agent relationship also causes fund managers to engage in other unusual practices. At the end of each quarter, prior to marketing the fund to potential new investors, fund managers often partake in a practice called 'window dressing', whereby the fund manager buys stocks that have recently performed well. The fund manager does this knowing that investors have a preference for investing in stocks that have recently performed strongly. Again, this practice adds to trends already present in the market, causing them to persist.

Lessons Learned

Firstly, our brain is hardwired to be influenced by the actions of others, this often has a tangible effect on the market.

Secondly, understanding the biases which influence trading decisions helps us to recognise when we are prone to making errors and also to understand why.

Thirdly, Scientific insights enable us to understand why, when markets are extremely cheap, investors may be so filled with fear and trepidation that they continue to sell rather than buy. Likewise, they enable us to predict the possibility that when markets are very expensive and rising strongly traders will chase the market higher, buying aggressively.

Fourthly, booms and busts and long term price trends are a recurring feature of markets because they are a reflection of the human psyche and the need for group conformity which causes investors to 'herd'. This behaviour can cause prices to reach extreme valuations.

Fifth, the workings of the fund management industry are not conducive to markets efficiently pricing assets since professional fund managers are often more focused on ensuring that their fund's performance hugs the market's performance.

Sixth, understanding how the human brain works and how it influences markets helps us understand why trend-following is such a successful strategy for traders. Understanding the rationale behind trend-following helps trend-following traders to succeed because they understand markets.

Finally, market collapses occur when the market is at an extreme valuation and a large number of traders share a confident sentiment about markets. Likewise, market bottoms occur when investor sentiment towards the market is extremely negative.

Introduction to the Following Chapters

A great deal of information has been covered so far. I have already outlined the main body of knowledge and skills that I acquired over the first 20 years of trading the markets which enabled much success. Most books would probably stop here, but this is an account of my trading journey, and I would be short-changing the reader if I were to end the book now because the journey hasn't finished. In fact, another leg was just beginning, because from 2010 onwards, as well as using trend-following, I became particularly interest in economics and politics and how they can be used to predict market movements.

Whilst consideration of political and economic factors doesn't dominate my approach to trading, both subjects played an increasingly important role in how I thought about markets. Not wanting to leave the reader stranded, the journey continues, but the terrain does become more difficult. I studied politics and economics and their influence on asset prices in the real life theatre of the market for least 20 hours per week, for the next six years, so this section does become somewhat more challenging. (I also became heavily involved in currency trading, but that is the subject for another book)

The following sections of this book form the icing on the trading cake and aren't essential, but they will help the trader determine the flavour of markets, and sense their direction. Trading is like most disciplines in that incremental gains become more and more difficult to acquire, the last ten percent being the most difficult. That is the point that we have now reached.

26. Macro Trading

The person with a narrow vision sees a narrow horizon

The person with a wide vision sees a wide horizon

(Ancient Maori saying)

In this section we widen the lens on our view of the world, seeing new information. We have looked at how earnings per share determine a stock's price, but now let's take another step backwards and examine the factors which determine how profitable companies will be, and hence what the value of shares will be. To do this we need to examine the health of the economy and the factors which influence it.

The economy in which companies operate is cyclical. For prolonged periods business conditions can be harsh, expansion can be difficult, even maintaining profitability can be a major challenge. But following tough periods economies tend to recover, profitability improves and opportunities to expand occur. Traders, in their desire to keep ahead of the market, are always seeking to identify when major changes in the investment environment will occur and trade to profit from these changes. To do this, investors monitor economic data and political developments, since these factors drive price trends in the value of stocks, bonds, commodities, and foreign exchange. This style of trading is called *macro trading*. Macro trading is defined by billionaire macro investor Stanley Drunckenmiller as "anticipating changes in economic trends that were not expected by others based on the assessment of economic and political factors" [6]

Many traders are unfamiliar with macro trading, instead they focus on catching short term fluctuations in the market, attracted by the idea of consistently catching small swings in the market. But there are a surprisingly small number of successful traders who operate this way. That's because small movements are notoriously difficult to consistently catch. Predicting when the rainy season will start is easier than predicting the onset of a short summer shower. That's why traders who target small moves in the market are few, and their lifespans as traders often short. If catching a large number of small moves were the best way to achieve high returns then hedge funds and pension funds would employ armies of traders, all scalping the markets, clocking up large gains by executing many quick trades. The fact that this is comparatively rare tells us definitively that superior returns aren't achieved this way. The most successful traders seek to identify significant movements in the market, using trend-following, economic data, and political analysis.

If the evidence for what constitutes a successful trading technique is defined by the size and scale of returns then macro trading is the king of trading strategies. It is used by almost every billionaire trader. In the case studies featured in several of the previous chapters we crossed from a trading methodology based on technical analysis into macro trading. In particular, these skills were used when trading metals and mining stocks because we considered the political and economic situation in China when making the trading decision. Furthermore, when trading during the European debt crisis the inclusion of political and economic factors proved to be crucial in formulating a successful trading strategy.

The purpose of the next section is to open the path to becoming a competent macro trader.

26.1 Macro Trading Skills

All macro trades still require the 3:1 risk reward ratio that was discussed in previous chapters, and trend-following principles remain valid. In addition, we wish to keep the trading strategy as simple as possible, but also to broaden our view, aiming to identify exceptional opportunities that might otherwise have been overlooked or underexploited if we were to just use technical analysis. When macro trading we consider government policy, the actions of central banks and economic data as well as any other relevant factors, seeking to identify where a potent cocktail of influences will trigger major price movements in the market.

Monetary Policy

Monetary policy is undertaken by central banks to influence the cost and availability of money. This is primarily done by adjusting interest rates. Interest rates are like the accelerator on a car, when they are pushed lower the carburettor opens up and allows more fuel into the engine, increasing its speed. Similarly, the increased flow of money from lower interest rates often causes the value of stocks and other assets such as housing to increase as more money enters the economy. One of the primary reasons for this is that banks and other financial institutions are increasingly willing to offer credit in the form of mortgages and loans on favourable terms as interest rates influence the prices of assets in another very important way, which is best explained using an example. A small investor has £10,000 to invest. Let's say that stocks give a return of 5% per year and that the interest rate being paid at the bank for deposits is 5%. In this situation the investor should choose to deposit the money in the bank, since the same return can be achieved, but the investor who deposits his £10,000 into the bank is not exposed to the risk of any losses, making the bank the best investment decision. Now let's say that the central bank reduces interest rates significantly, causing the bank to have to reduce the interest rate it offers to savers. The bank now only offers an interest rate of 1%, whereas the stock market still offers a return of 5%. Although the investor is exposed to the risk of losses in the stock market, it now looks much more attractive than when interest rates were 5%, we should therefore expect falling interest rates to cause stock prices to rise as investors move money from low yielding deposits into higher yielding stocks.

The stock market's value is primarily influenced by the actions of big players, these are the pension funds and major investment houses. They have such huge amounts of money that bank deposits are unsuitable. The benchmark that they use to determine the risk free rate of return is the yield on the 10- year government bond, because it is considered a very low risk investment. It's is almost completely risk free because default is rare, but its price is greatly influenced by the interest rate set by the central bank. We will next look at a method used by major investors to calculate which asset class they should invest in.

26.2 The Yield Gap

The yield gap indicator provides a rule of thumb to determine whether stocks are cheap compared to the risk free rate of return. This is done by comparing the yield on the 10-year government bond to the dividend yield on stocks. When the dividend yield on stocks is above the yield on the 10-year government bond then stocks are signalled to be good value. As an example, for a U.K investor, the current yield on the 10- year bond is 1.5%, compared to a yield of 4.1% on the stocks in the FTSE 100. Therefore, because the yield on stocks is above that of 10-year government bonds this indicator shows that stocks are cheap compared to bonds. As a macro trader this indicator signals to buy stocks in anticipation of other investors moving money from lower yielding asset classes such as bonds into the stock market. However, because we are using multiple trading filters, such as trend-following, this would only be done if our other criteria are also met.

26.3 The Equity Risk Premium

It is common sense that investors should demand a higher rate of return to invest in stocks than in risk free investments such as government bonds. How much extra yield investor's demand for investing in stocks compared to risk free investments is called the equity risk premium. During periods of panic stock prices fall. One reason for this is that investors fear that forthcoming events will cause company earnings to contract, and therefore stock prices to fall. At these times investors frequently become overly fearful and share prices fall too far, causing the yield on stocks to rise. When the yield on stocks is much higher than the yield on government 10-year bonds the equity risk premium is said to be high. In trades I have described previously there have been several instances where the equity risk premium reached extremes, signalling excellent buying opportunities. One instance occurred after the crash in 2001 when investors feared a major recession, another occurred in 2008 during a major recession. Investors who bought at these times made large returns because they anticipated that the recessions would pass. Throughout the recessions company dividends were cut only slightly yet the average share price fell by 40% and because the share prices fell but the dividend yield remained high, stocks became cheap. Furthermore, the recession caused interest rates to be cut aggressively. Once the recession passed, investor confidence returned and investor's funds flowed back into the stock market because the equity risk premium had become extremely large, causing the level of the stock market to rise strongly as a tide of money flowed back into the cheap stock market.

Investors could predict this move on the basis that the equity risk premium had reached extreme levels and that stocks would form major new trends lasting many years as stock prices climbed to return to more normal valuations. Having this knowledge helps investors know that the new uptrends which formed after the market crashed are likely to be substantial and that buying and holding quality stocks is the best strategy.

26.4 Understanding central banks and interest rates

A key aspect of macro trading is to understand the actions of central banks, and why they adjust interest rates. One way to explain this is to use an analogy of a simplified economy since this enables much of the complexity of actual economics to be excluded. A commonly used analogy is the real life example of a babysitting co-op. This small group, and the way in which they exchange their services is representative of an economy and provides us with many of the important insights that we need to learn to understand central banking and economics.

26.5 The babysitting co-op

A group of people agree to babysit for one another, forming a babysitting co-op. Couples are required to do a reciprocal amount of babysitting to that which they receive. To ensure fairness the babysitting co-op devised a solution. They issued coupons - pieces of paper equivalent to one hour of babysitting time. Babysitters received the appropriate number of coupons directly from other babysitters, making the system self-enforcing. As long as the babysitters were reliable, what could go wrong?

It turned out that there was a technical problem. Think about the coupon holdings of a typical couple. During periods when they had few occasions to go out the couple would probably try to build up a reserve, then run that reserve down when occasions arose to go out. There would be an averaging out of these demands. One couple would be going out when another was staying at home. But since many couples would be holding reserves of coupons at any given time the co-op needed to have a decent amount of coupons in circulation.

But an unforeseen problem occurred. The number of coupons in circulation became low. As a result, most couples were anxious to add to their reserves by babysitting and became reluctant to spend coupons. But one couple's decision to go out was another's chance to babysit; thus it became difficult to earn coupons. Knowing this, couples became increasingly reluctant to use their reserves, reducing babysitting opportunities still further. In short, the co-op fell into a recession. People had become pessimistic about their future opportunities to acquire coupons and so they reduced spending, causing the economy of the babysitting co-op to grind to a halt, much like in real economic recessions when low levels of economic activity occur and money circulates more slowly, causing other people to lose confidence and reduce spending, further slowing the economy.

In this real life example many members of the co-op were lawyers, and in the hope of spurring more going out and hence the faster circulation of coupons, they passed a rule requiring each couple to go out at least twice a month. But this wasn't popular. Fortunately, some of the people in the co-op were economists and they proposed a different approach. They proposed issuing more coupons so that people had plentiful reserves, this was expected to raise confidence, causing them to spend more. Couples did become more willing to go out, opportunities to babysit multiplied, and everyone was happy.

The example shows what happens during recessions. People become pessimistic causing others to also become pessimistic. This initiates a slowdown in economic activity which is to everyone's detriment. Yet during recessions the ability for the system to produce the services that everybody wants remains present and undiminished. Technically all that is required is for more coupons to be issued, giving people the confidence to spend. That is why confidence is critical to economic health. For example, suppose that the U.S. stock market was to crash, threatening to undermine consumer confidence. Would this inevitably mean a disastrous recession? Think of it this way: When consumer confidence declines, it is as if for some reason the typical member of the co-op had become less willing to go out, and has become more anxious to accumulate coupons for a rainy day. This could indeed lead to a slump - but need not if management were alert and responded by issuing more coupons. That is exactly what the central banks do when they anticipate a recession. Suppose the central bank did not respond quickly enough and the economy slumps, there is still normally no need for panic, the situation can be rectified by pumping more money into the economy, giving people the confidence to spend.

Periodically economies can go into a deep slump. In these instances printing more coupons doesn't work because confidence is extremely depressed, causing the circulation to slow to a trickle, yet the members still want to go out and are still willing to fulfil their baby sitting duties adequately. To resolve this problem the co-op could allow members to borrow extra coupons from the management in times of need, repaying with the coupons received from subsequent babysitting. To prevent members from abusing this privilege however, the management could impose a penalty - requiring borrowers to repay more coupons than they borrowed. Under this new system, couples would hold smaller reserves of coupons, knowing they could borrow more if necessary. The co-op's officers would, however, have acquired a new tool of management. If members of the co-op reported it was easy to find babysitters and hard to find opportunities to babysit, the terms under which members could borrow coupons could be made more favourable, encouraging more people to go out. If babysitters were scarce, those terms could be worsened, encouraging people to go out less. In other words, this more sophisticated co-op would have the equivalent of a central bank, it could stimulate a depressed economy by reducing the interest rate and cool off an overheated one by raising it.

Lessons Learned

Firstly, pension funds and major investors move markets. Knowing the criteria that they use to determine the attractiveness of a market helps traders to front run their actions, buying before the funds buy and enjoying the subsequent price rise.

Secondly, interest rates exert a powerful force on stock prices, not just because they influence economic activity, but because they set the risk free rate of return.

Thirdly, there are many factors that can influence an economy. The confidence of consumers and business to spend and invest is critical. Confidence is difficult to measure and even more difficult to predict, hence economic forecasts are always subject to uncertainty.

Finally, central banks have a powerful influence over the economy and their actions are a significant driving force in the economy and the markets. The influence and actions of central banks on financial markets are discussed in more detail in the next section.

Central Banks and Quantitative Easing (QE)

Sometimes economies fall into the deepest of slumps and interest rates cannot be cut further. To provide additional stimulus to get the economy moving again QE is used. QE encompasses a number of methods to stimulate the economy. Each measure is reliant upon the exclusive privilege of the central bank to issue and print new money. This is intended to have the same effect as printing more coupons had on the economy of the babysitting co-op. During a program of QE assets are bought using new money that the central bank has issued, leaving the previous owners of the assets with the freshly minted cash from the central bank. This money has to be spent or invested, it then generates increased economic activity. As an example, the central bank in the United States, as part of its QE program, created new money and bought government bonds. The investors who sold their government bonds to the central bank were given new money in return. The investors needed to put to work this newly acquired money to earn a return, so they invest the money in businesses or other assets. This increases economic activity, generating demand and raising confidence in the future prospects for the economy to generate wealth and prosperity.

Quantitative easing also has a number of important 'side effects' that are positive for an economy.

1) Confidence – Investor confidence is heightened by the presence of a large buyer in the market, this helps support asset prices. If for example the central bank decided to use QE to mint new funds to invest in the stock market then the presence of a large buyer such as a central bank supports prices, making the asset less risky, triggering increasing demand and rising prices. Rising asset prices have the additional benefit of reducing bad debts, making it easier for companies to secure new financing and encouraging new investment.

2) Policy signalling – The central bank has the option to state that it will hold interest rates lower for a prolonged period, meaning investors have a high degree of certainty that interest rates will remain low, triggering money to be moved into higher yielding riskier assets, raising their value, causing a wealth effect that will increase economic growth.

3) Portfolio rebalancing – because QE causes the interest rates on safe investments such as bank deposits and government bonds to fall to very low levels this pushes investors into riskier investments offering higher returns such as making new loans to business, investing in property, stocks or corporate debt, which increases economic activity.

4) Market liquidity – large investors are more likely to buy assets if there is an active market that can accommodate their large trades. When a central bank enters the market the presence of such a large buyer increases market liquidity, meaning that the

large trades that pensions funds and other financial institutions need to do can be done more readily.

5) Money –The increased amount of money in the financial system from quantitative easing cause's banks to relax their standards for new loans, making credit cheaper and more available, which stimulates economic activity.

6) QE - is a process of 'printing' new currency, increasing the quantity in circulation. A typical outcome of QE is therefore to diminish a currency's value, resulting in a lower exchange rate, making goods and services more competitive in international markets, stimulating export demand, creating additional economic growth.

The policies of the central bank and the government target demand in the economy to match capacity, so that resources do not lie idle. The central bank assesses their performance by monitoring the rate of inflation because inflation is the rate at which the price of goods and services in the economy are rising. Demand in an economy is sufficient if prices are rising by 2% per year, hence most central banks in Europe target an inflation rate of 2% per annum. If inflation is rising faster than this amount for a sustained period then it is often indicative of excessive demand and action may need to be taken to slow economic growth.

Macro Trading in Action

In the next section we will look at several examples of macro trading, firstly by examining a trading opportunity that arose in Europe which was identified using the macro trading methodology, and another example in which macro trading signals indicate that an attractive trading opportunity may arise in the Japanese market in the future.

Trading Europe

There is a strong rationale to support the idea that Europe is a fertile ground for the occurrence of asset price booms and busts. The reason for its heightened susceptibility is that the European financial system is unique. The Eurozone is a group of countries which share a common currency (the euro). Therefore all countries using the euro must have the same interest rate. However, the economic strength of each nation within Europe differs widely making this a flawed arrangement which is likely to cause some nations to have economic booms, since the interest rate will be too low; whilst for others interest rates will be too high, causing economic stagnation. This distortion, caused by the introduction of the single currency, triggered the Eurozone's first major economic crisis in 2010, when the boom in property prices which had occurred in some parts of Europe, busted. Next we examine the causes of this crisis in greater detail because the factors which caused the crisis remain, and another cycle of boom and bust could recur, presenting attractive trading opportunities.

26.5 Europe's Economic Crisis

The precursor to the Eurozone's first major economic crisis was divergent economic performance between nations within the Eurozone. Export orientated countries such as Germany were highly exposed to slowing global growth, and were struggling to avoid recession. The European Central Bank used low interest rates to promote economic growth in the slow growing nations, but the blanket low interest rate across Europe had a powerful and unwanted side effect; it fuelled a huge movement of cheap money into countries such as Spain and Ireland sparking a surge of investment in property, triggering a boom in property prices. This occurred because these economies were experiencing stronger economic growth, driven by a buoyant housing market. The flood of cheap money was akin to adding more alcohol to the punch bowl when the party was already swinging. Rising property prices attracted additional inflows of speculative money, accelerating the price rises. Property boomed. people got rich, others joined in, perpetuating the boom.

The introduction of the single currency played another vital role in the boom. It allowed speculative money to move across Europe to invest in the booming property sector without risk of loss on currency transactions. The factors which caused this boom bust cycle remain intact making me mindful that a similar event could recur, presenting an outstanding trading opportunity.

Rationale for another Economic Boom within Europe.

During the past 30 years the mountain of debt in Europe has grown to record levels. This debt needs to be reduced. Paying debts takes money out of the economy that would otherwise have been spent on goods and services, so that when nations are paying down large national debts economic growth is slower. To counteract this interest rates will be kept low. We know this because historically the drag from paying down large debt piles results in periods of ultra-low interest rates, often lasting decades.

Looking forward, I knew two powerful forces would be in action within the European economy. Firstly, interest rates would be very low for a long time, meaning a low risk free rate of return. Secondly, Europe is made up of widely differing economies and very low interest rates might be unsuitable for the stronger economies, triggering a boom. These two macro factors formed the basis of a trade to invest in German property. This is the subject of the next section of the book.

Investing in Germany

The strongest economy in Europe was Germany, making it least suited to the low interest rate medicine being applied by the European Central Bank to cure faltering economic growth in weak economies such as Greece. I figured that this meant Germany was the country most likely to enjoy an economic boom. I thought the two sectors of the German economy most likely to boom were the property sector and the stock market.

I first analysed the German property sector, with the starting point for the enquiry being the examination of several property company annual reports, since they provided a speedy insight into the property market. German property companies stated in their reports that they were investing in property yielding 7-10% per year. The risk free rate of return in Germany at that time was below 1%. The gap between the risk free rate of return and that of the relatively safe return of 7% in property appeared excessively wide, therefore it seemed reasonable to anticipate that investors would move money from risk free investments into property to capture the yield differential, causing property prices to rise as new money flooded in. Property companies would gain from rising property prices as well as receiving their rental yield, boosting their profitability. If property prices rose 10% per year and had a rental yield of 8% that would be a total return of 18%. With a risk free rate of return of less than 1% property could attract huge new inflows if prices rose strongly, fuelling the boom, accelerating the price increases, and offering the potential for outstanding returns.

Having used macro factors such as low interest rates and a wide yield differential between assets to identify a potential boom, the idea needed to be cross checked against the markets' opinion. If the property sector had underperformed the market then it could be a warning sign that I had misanalysed the situation. I expected the sector to have been strong, informing me that other investors agreed with my reasoning. The property sector had indeed outperformed the stock market. Both the stock market and the property sector were in powerful uptrends, signalling stocks should be bought. The next step was to identify the best property stocks using an analysis of earnings growth rates and relative strength. Google Finance proved a very useful tool for this. By entering the name of one company into the search engine it produced a list of similar companies, enabling the relative strength of a large number of German property companies to be compared. Analysis identified a stock called TAG Immobilien. It had high relative strength, rising over 300% in the previous four years, but still traded at a market average P/E ratio (the company's growth rate was obtained from digitallook.co.uk).

Fig. 28 *Chart of TAG Immobilien, Demonstrating an Excellent Trading Opportunity*

The buy signal occurred when the price broke out from the narrow trading range, above 930. A stop loss was placed at the prior lows, at 900, giving a downside risk of 4% if the breakout failed. On the two prior occasions when this stock had consolidated and formed a trading range the breakout from that trading range saw the share price rapidly increase 25%. Therefore it is reasonable to anticipate a move of similar proportions if a breakout were to occur again. The trade proved successful and, as anticipated, the price increased quickly. However the potential for a boom in German property diminished because economic problems in emerging markets meant lower demand for German exports, slowing the key export sector of the economy and lessening the likelihood of the economy overheating, so the trade was closed. However, the probability of a property boom developing continues to remain, albeit at a much reduced likelihood.

Japan

Japan faces major economic difficulties. It has a mountainous debt pile and an aging population. In fact, Japan's population has a higher average age than any country in history, and it is still growing quickly, with 25% of people aged over 65. Japan's aging population is so large and so old that it is the first nation to use more adult nappies than children's nappies.

Aging populations have expensive healthcare needs and costly pension demands. But Japan has another major economic problem festering. It has accumulated one of the largest debt piles in history, yet its capacity for repayment is declining as its population shrinks and greys. This has global implications; failure to repay its debts would trigger the largest debt default in history. It would also make investor's doubt the ability of several European nations to repay their debts, since they also have large debts and aging populations.

To understand how to trade future eventualities in the Japanese markets it is first wise to examine Japan's past to understand how the country got into such a mess, followed by reviewing the solution proposed by Japan's government.

The Japanese Boom

During the 1980's the Japanese economy developed an enormous financial bubble. At its peak a small area of Tokyo where the imperial palace stood was estimated to have a greater value than the entire real estate of California. By 1990 the bubble had peaked. Shortly thereafter a vicious bust developed. The government didn't recognise the bursting of the bubble and continued to cool the economy, inadvertently tipping it deep into a slump. Banks incurred heavy losses from bad loans, and remained saddled with mountainous debts. The bad debts created a zombie economy which barely functioned. This lasted for almost 20 years. During this time the Japanese government spent huge amounts of money to kick-start growth, but it never recovered sufficiently to return the nation to economic health.

The bursting of one of the largest financial bubbles in history and the ensuing slump burdened Japan with debts of over 1 Quadrillion Yen. These debts are over 20 times as large as the government's tax revenue. Japan is at high risk of defaulting on its debt, but it has survived so far because the government has utilised its citizens'abundant savings to fund debt repayment. However, the day of reckoning is rapidly approaching because Japan's aging population need their savings to fund their retirement. With each year that passes, the possibility of defaulting grows as more hardworking Japanese retire and tap into their pension funds, leaving a reducing pool of money available for debt repayment.

In 2008 Japan's politicians devised policies to offset the oncoming crisis. After a period of political turmoil which saw three finance ministers leave their post in quick succession, a new set of political hands were elected. They discarded the usual methods of consensus building that characterised Japan's style of government in favour of an aggressive plan dubbed 'monetary shock and awe.' The new leaders implemented a series of radical policies, the most important policy required the Bank of Japan to initiate a huge programme of QE to stimulate economic growth and raise inflation to 2%. But, like all brave economic policies, it entailed serious risks. Inflation at 2% could cause an exodus from savings accounts and the bond market, since paying savers interest rates of 0.5% whilst inflation was at 2% meant savers money would lose 1.5% of spending power every year. If this happened the government would lose access to the funds it had been using to repay debts. The QE program does offer some protection against panicking investors. QE enables the government to print new money to finance its own spending, removing the risk of a shortfall. But the fact that such huge volumes would need to be printed to plug the gap if savers withdrew funds poses major risks for the health of the currency.

Printing huge amounts of new money diminishes the value of the existing currency. The Japanese currency has fallen from 80 yen to the dollar to 122 yen per Dollar, a near 50% drop, creating a highly tradable trend. The government's policies have also triggered a sharp move higher in the stock market, with the market more than doubling since the QE program began, showing that investors are already moving money into the stock market to protect their wealth.

To understand the potential longer term effects from Japan's huge QE program and the possible end game for the resolution of Japan's financial problems we can use the ideas from previous chapters about how things can transition away from stability very suddenly, similar to what occurs during an avalanche, when the pent up forces of instability are suddenly unleashed. In relation to Japan, we know that the economy hasn't experienced a major economic crisis for 25 years, meanwhile debt has become mountainous. A heightened potential exists for Japan to experience a major financial crisis and this will most likely result in large trends in Japanese markets as huge amounts of money move. Technical analysis will help to predict the timing, and the boom bust model will assist greatly in trading the displacement.

Possible outcomes in Japan can also be understood by looking at past outcomes for countries with extremely large debts that have resorted to printing new money to repay debts rather than the traditional method of using tax revenue. In countries where investors believe they are at risk of suffering a collapse in the value of the currency, one of the first things to happen is that astute investors who foresee the oncoming crisis transfer funds abroad. By doing so investors sell the currency that they expect to depreciate, buying stronger foreign currencies so that they no longer own the vulnerable currency. When the crisis expires they rebuy their home currency, often at a much lower rate, and snap up investments at bargain prices.

Investors who are not out of the currency at the onset of the crisis can still take action to protect, and even enhance their wealth. One way is to invest in property, or in the stock market. The ethos behind both of these investment decisions is the same. When you buy something with cash you buy something that has real value. The central bank cannot produce new companies or buildings; it can only print new money. For example, when buying a property, you exchange money for the property. This insulates the buyer of the property from further falls in the value of money. Property prices have a strong tendency to rise when citizens lose faith in the currency. Japans QE program has supported property prices, but its biggest effect has been on the stock market.

Stocks have many qualities that make them a highly suitable investment in the environment that Japan may face in the future. Since the start of QE stocks have rocketed over 100% in three years, making Japan one of the best performing markets in the world, providing evidence that savvy investors knew QE would devalue their savings and had already started moving to protect their wealth.

It remains a possibility that this is only the first phase of a much larger and more powerful movement. However key developments need to occur before entering the Japanese market since Japan may struggle to escape the deflationary trap that it is in.

One possible road map for how events could unfold is obtained by examining the events that occurred in the Zimbabwean economy. It has endured extreme economic problems and debts that it could not repay using the normal means of tax revenue. Instead it resorted to printing new money to repay its debts. Zimbabwe provides insights for trading a crisis in Japan because investors lost confidence in Zimbabwe's currency. Zimbabwe's economic crisis started in the late 1990's and saw the value of its currency collapse. In one of the most extreme currency collapses ever to occur Zimbabwe's currency became almost worthless. One hundred trillion Zimbabwean dollars became worth $1 U.S.

Fig 29. *A Currency Note of Zimbabwe*

To escape the plunging currency investors ploughed funds into the stock market. In the 12 months to April 2007 the Zimbabwean stock market rose 12,000% as the value of the currency collapsed. In fact, the stock market rose 3 times as much as inflation. We can deduce from this, and from other instances where the currency depreciates sharply, that investing in stocks provides excellent returns even whilst the economy and the currency collapses. Zimbabweans also rushed to invest in property. An article in the Zimbabwean Herald Newspaper notes, 'properties prices rose by between 42 000 percent and 110 000 percent in the previous 12 months to 2008.

Zimbabwe provides an example of what happens when confidence in the currency fails; soaring property and stock markets are the norm rather than the exception. Whilst something this extreme in Japan is highly unlikely it is not unreasonable to be alert to the possibility that the value of Japan's currency may at some point be heavily diluted by the printing of new money, triggering a boom in stock prices and property prices. This can only happen if Japan succeeds in breaking out of its current deflationary spiral.

The history of economic crises not only reminds us of outcomes, it can also influence the outcome of future debt crises. That's because history is studied to provide insights into how future events will be resolved. As an example, Thucydides wrote the only major contemporary history of the Peloponnesian war at the end of the 5th century B.C. What can we learn from this? Greece is a tiny country; the war cannot have any real effect on our lives today, everybody who fought in it is long dead, the battles forgotten about and the cities that were fought over have crumbled to dust. Almost all that remains of the Peloponnesian war is Thucydides account of it. Yet that account is still important because Thucydides writings continued shaping events. Leaders in later eras read Thucydides and when encountering a similar situation were influenced by his writings. Financial crises are no different to instances of war. Previous financial crises influence the outcome of future financial crises because investors use historic instances as a road map to predict and navigate future opportunities and threats, influencing the course of events.

It is likely that the powerful trends that have occurred recently in the Japanese markets have at least partially arisen because investors have studied history. They are moving money in anticipation of events that their studies have told them may occur as Japan seeks resolution of its economic problems. That doesn't mean there won't be bumps along the road, but Japan's debt problem must be resolved either through repayment or default. Repayment is looking an increasing remote possibility that could only be achieved via the issuing of huge quantities of new money that history has shown could initiate large trends in the currency and stock market. Default is nearly always a less favourable option.

Lessons Learned

Firstly, A knowledge of macroeconomic data and economic history maximises the chances of recognising where large trends will occur, enabling the trader to focus resources on superior opportunities.

Secondly, In the book Reminiscences of a Stock Operator, the trader Larry Livingstone writes 'But my greatest discovery was that a man must study general conditions, to size them up so as to anticipate probabilities' Livingston had used his new-found insight to predict a large market move, to devastating effect, and writes 'I was worth over one million after the close of business that day. But my biggest winnings were not in dollars but in intangibles: I had been right, I had looked ahead and followed a clear cut plan. I had learned what a man must do in order to make big money; I was out of the gambler class; I had learned to trade intelligently in a big way. It was a day of days for me.'

27. Better Forecasting

Forecasting is an important part of trading. Surprisingly, most of us are experienced forecasters, we just don't know it. That's because every day we make forecasts, sometimes they are important and require careful consideration, but many are done so routinely that they don't even enter our consciousness. For example, on hearing about roadworks that could affect our journey to work we combine that information with information about weather conditions and our day's schedule, and then quickly reassess our forecast for what time we will need to start our journey. On other occasions we need to forecast the weather, so we examine the clouds, check if other people are wearing coats and consider the weather patterns over recent days, then make a decision. These are the everyday forecasts that occur with minimal thought, yet they work amazing well. These forecasts are made using a particular part of the brain, utilising pathways that have evolved to provide quick decisions. The ability to make these rapid decisions is an evolutionary trait that helps us cope with everyday life and not become bogged down with overanalysing every small decision that we have to make. This fast method of making predictions and decisions is achieved by using a pathway in the brain called system 1.

There is another pathway in the brain that is used for making more complex decisions. This pathway is used when a deeper analysis of problems is required. Scientists unimaginatively call this pathway system 2. System 2 thinking is deeper, slower, effortful and logic based thinking. It critically examines information to reach a decision. System 2 thinking is the type that traders should utilise when making a decision, yet often don't. That's because sometimes decisions seem intuitively correct, making the impetus to deeply analyse the information seem unnecessary. This frequently causes costly miscalculations.

Pattern seeking

System 1 thinking is so habitual in our everyday lives that its use is often subconscious. Also, we often uncritically accept information that is formed by others using system 1 thinking. For example, during an unusually cold period at the start of winter it is not uncommon to read newspaper headlines that weather forecasters have changed their predictions and that they now expect the forthcoming winter to be the coldest in 50 years. Or, following a strong rally in the stock market, we frequently read that analysts are upgrading their forecasts for the level at which the market will finish the year.

These forecasts are based on taking recent information and extrapolating it into the future. Such forecasts are accepted because at the time they seem intuitively correct. This is because our brains and our senses have evolved this way. Our days as hunter-gathers have trained us to believe that if food is scarce we should plan that it will continue to be scarce, enabling better provisioning of food, enhancing our survival prospects. The repeated occurrence of events which favoured the survival of humans with pattern seeking has caused it to become one of the most strongly held human traits. We would find everyday life bewildering without it. But in some people pattern seeking behaviour has reached extreme proportions, leading them to form unusual beliefs. Michael Shermer, writing in the Scientific American magazine[5], questions why some people hear voices in random sounds generated by electronic devices, or why people formulate conspiracy theories about events, such as believing that the Queen of the United Kingdom plotted the death of Princess Diana. He concludes that scientific evidence confirms that pattern seeking is hardwired into our brains, and that it is difficult to supress, especially in complex situations. Added to this, humans are intensely social animals and we are inclined to accept beliefs if they have a fitting narrative and are widely accepted as being truthful.

Behaviour and markets

This widespread use of the intuitive and rapid system 1 thinking is the primary reason why the history of financial markets is filled with manias and panics. Ideas spawned using system 1 thinking seep into markets and then spread into the media. They then grow and become generally accepted beliefs. A rising market adds credence to positive beliefs and increases the chatter about the phenomenon. The more a belief is accepted the more likely it is to be believed by others. After rising strongly as a result of the faulty belief the market then crashes as the faults in the belief are revealed. What seemed intuitively correct is exposed as being a flawed understanding of reality, and panic develops as the market slides even lower.

One of the largest errors of thought to occur as a result of system 1 thinking happened when investors came to believe that the U.S housing market was stable. Investors arrived at this decision because from 1975-2005 home prices in the United States never fell across all regions. Dips in home prices were modest and localised. This prolonged period of stability grew into an assumption that because a synchronised decline in U.S house prices hadn't happened for a long time it had a low probability of ever occurring. The forecasts that the housing market would only ever suffer minor setbacks became more widely believed the longer house prices increased. Investor's use of System 1 thinking was the real culprit behind one of the largest financial crashes in history, costing trillions of dollars in lost wealth.

The use of our ability to make rapid decisions based on things that seem intuitively correct has lead us into major difficulties on other occasions. Another notable instance was when the United States Government asked the CIA whether Saddam Hussain's Iraq had weapons of mass destruction. In one report the CIA stated with absolute certainty that Iraq had weapons of mass destruction. No such weapons were found. It was a classic example of how the CIA's judgement was influenced by Saddam Hussain's unusual behaviour. Saddam exhibited behaviour that was akin to someone who was hiding something, and they interpreted this as meaning he was concealing weapons of mass destruction. This was a classic example of the quick thinking that takes place using system 1 causing sub-par decision making. Critical analysis of the evidence would have led to the conclusion that despite hundreds of inspections they actually didn't have any compelling evidence to refute Saddam's claim not to have the weapons.

If there was one positive that came out of the misguided invasion of Iraq it was that it triggered a full review of the CIA's forecasting ability. With an annual budget of $60 billion and an army of analysts and insider sources across the globe it is reasonable to have expected them to be able to determine if Iraq possessed weapons of mass destruction. The CIA's blunder cost over 11,000 lives and hundreds of billions of dollars. The CIAs forecasting capability needed to be improved. The review of the service lead to the largest and most in-depth study into forecasting ever conducted and provided invaluable insights into how we can improve our forecasts.

Improving forecasting

The review of the CIA started with tests to benchmark the forecasting ability of the agency. People from ordinary backgrounds as well as those with specialist backgrounds were invited to take part in a forecasting challenge and test their skills against the CIA. The tests consisted of forecasting the outcome of future world events. Volunteers competed in making predictions about a wide range of happenings, covering topics such as what the price of oil would be in 12 months' time, to naming the candidate who would win a presidential race. To ensure that the test reflected the reality of real world forecasting the contestants were able to update their forecasts as new events and information came to the fore. The assessors diligently logged the updates to assess how prediction accuracy changed as the time to the event being predicted neared.

What was the outcome of the experiment? A significant number of amateur forecasters consistently beat the professionals by a wide margin. Within the group of high performing forecasters were a small group of people who consistently obtained results far in excess of average. These forecasters were elite forecasters.

Elite forecasters

The vast majority of elite forecasters had no previous experience as professional forecasters. Statistical analysis showed the results of elite forecasters were beyond what was ever likely to be obtained by being lucky. With the experiment revealing all that the assessors had hoped for, they now needed to acquire the secrets to forecasting from the elite forecasters. They examined the data about when forecasts were updated, and the magnitude of each update. They also thoroughly examined how they analysed questions to assess their methodology for forecasting, as well as investigating how they selected and utilised evidence.

They learned that one of the crucial aspects which defined an elite forecaster was how they approached questions. A shared characteristic was that as a first step they broke down the question into several sub-questions. They then answered the sub questions and used the answers to gain the information to solve the primary question. Let's now look at an example of this methodology.

Elite Forecasters in Action

If elite forecasters were given the question: - Will the price of oil be between $50 and $60 per barrel in 6 months' time? How would they answer it? Perhaps surprisingly they didn't primarily focus on analysing the oil market. Instead they broke the main question down into sub questions: -

- What is the current price of oil?

- Thinking about the difference between the current oil price and the target price range of $50 to $60 they would assess how much the oil price would have to move to enter the target range. They would then assess how frequently price moves of that magnitude occur and how long these movements take.

- They considered such things as how much time in the past 50 years oil traded in the $50 to $60 price range and use this information to devise a statistical probability that oil will be trading in that range in 12 months' time.

- They would find out what the mean inflation adjusted price of oil has been over the past 100 years and consider this information.

- They also learnt methods to predict price moves in commodities including trend-following and technical analysis, and applied these methods.

The idea of answering questions by formulating other sub questions is not unique to the elite forecasters. An Italian born physicist called Enrico Fermi, who had an important role in the development of the atom bomb, was famous for his ability to use this technique to answer complex questions. In his lectures he would tease his students with questions that would require them to use this technique. His Wikipedia page details his favourite brain teasing question to pose to his students. The question was "how many piano tuners are there in Chicago?"

After flummoxing his students Fermi would demonstrate how to answer the question. The first stage was to break down the question into sub questions so as to answer the question in stages:

- estimate the number of pianos in Chicago by considering how many homes, business, schools and concert halls have pianos

- find out how frequently a piano requires tuning

- determine the time it takes to tune a piano

- estimate the average number of hours a piano tuner works

Thinking through this process, which often entailed further breaking down of these questions into other sub questions produces astoundingly accurate predictions. The ability to solve problems in this way is highly valued and has caused companies such as Google and Microsoft to regularly pose this type of question to job candidates.

The ability to make high calibre predictions was also found to be linked to other attributes.

Firstly, and perhaps most importantly, several studies have shown that people with great forecasting skills and the ability to grasp new skills quickly have open mind-sets. This meant that they view the future as having multiple possibilities, none of them certain. They continually strove to find new information that supported or challenged their beliefs and so they were constantly reviewing and fine tuning their opinions.

Secondly, they considered information from a wide variety of sources and welcomed finding evidence that challenged their current viewpoint just as much as they valued unearthing evidence supporting their existing forecast. They had an overall outlook on the world which suggested they thought the world was filled with uncertainty and change. They believed that outcomes are always uncertain and that they didn't know the truth with certainty.

Thirdly, they thought about problems in a self-critical way: They habitually analysed and re analysed evidence from many different angles, reinterpreting the evidence from varying perspectives, constantly reviewing and reflecting on information and the way they have processed it, searching for faults in the evidence and in their thinking. Having seen the investment case made by some of the world's best traders for trades they believe will be profitable I have noticed the same analytical skills being used. Evidence is critically analysed and tested. The breadth-of-thought is wide-ranging. This challenges most people's image of successful fund managers as being arrogant, aggressive and brimming with self-confidence. This is a media created image that has no grounding in reality. Most are deep thinkers, their sentences filled with reflection and their thoughts express awareness of many possible outcomes.

Lessons Learned

Firstly, how we think is a critical and often overlooked ingredient for successful trading. The characteristics that define elite forecasters tallies strongly with the characteristics of successful traders, after all, the disciplines are closely related. Interviews with top traders have repeatedly highlighted that a key factor characterising successful traders is the critical and reflective thought processes that occur when using system 2 thinking. Elite traders are constantly seeking to avoid decisions that stem from the fast, intuitive, emotional and bias ridden decisions emanating from system 1 thinking. In fact, elite traders consciously seek to identify when the market is filled with an opinion that has been derived from system 1 thinking, knowing that when the market realises it is wrong a tradable move will occur as the market corrects.

Secondly, elite forecasters are open to learning new skills. When faced with offbeat challenges such as predicting the price of oil or who would win an election in an obscure country they embraced the opportunity to acquire new skills and knowledge.

Thirdly, the insights used by elite forecasters suggests that the traits for making outstanding predictions are transferable and can be learned. Methods such as Fermi's technique of breaking questions down to answerable bits and then adding up the bits to provide the answer to complex problems are highly useful skills for traders to acquire. (See his Wikipedia page for other examples of his techniques).

Fourthly, traders must seek to filter out the powerful biases on our trading decisions otherwise we risk being constantly wrong footed. Markets are a paradox. What becomes conventional wisdom is nearly always wrong and is nearly always discounted in the market. System 1 thinking will almost always lead our decisions to be swayed by this faulty evidence. Instead, independent thought and effortful critical thinking involving multi-dimensional analysis and reanalysis of evidence must be used. These characteristics are the hallmarks of good system 2 thinking. They are the hallmarks of elite traders.

Fifth, Karl Popper said 'True ignorance is not the absence of knowledge but the refusal to acquire it.' The internet has made available tremendous amounts of information which should be fully utilised to ensure that we know as much as possible about both sides of the trade before formulating an opinion. Google Alerts is an excellent free service that will routinely scan the web for information enabling traders to effortlessly collate information on any subject from a wide variety of sources. Using services such as Google Alerts allows us to make a big step forward in acquiring the breadth of information necessary to make great decisions, and help eliminate any conscious or subconscious filtering of information that we search for.

Conclusion

'Come writer and critics who prophesize with your pen, and keep your eyes wide the chance won't come again, and don't speak too soon for the wheels still in spin, and there's no tellin' who that is namin', for the loser now will be later to win, for the times they area a-changin'

Bob Dylan, The Times They Are a-Changin'

Change washes the old, and brings in the new. For traders, this cycle provides a constant flow of new material to analyse and assess. The continuous flow of the new will bring with it tremendous trading opportunities, as will the fall of the old. The flux of history will never expire, and so the trader will never be without opportunity.

In this book I hope to have communicated some ideas that will be cause for thought, and also to have imparted some time tested methodologies for trading success. I expect that, on buying this book, some expected to read a text that talked about a long series of very successful trades, like a Don Bradman innings, masterfully scoring a bag full of runs without error, rather than accounts concerning a series of market movements that knocked my helmet off, leaving me pummelled and bruised, only to bat on. Yet the necessities for becoming a successful trader are no different to succeeding at business or sport. No one is so gifted as to not need to learn tough lessons in the market, and success would not have been so rewarding if it were easy. I also imagine that the book would have bored readers should I have chosen to document a long series of winning trades, for they would contain few insights or dramas, and hence offer little preparation for the market that awaits.

With regard to technical information, I hope to have conveyed my enthusiasm for using price as a key indicator, since my aim was to show that the market price is the ultimate arbiter of whether a trade is good or bad, and that price also exhibits all of the characteristics of simplicity and accuracy required for making good trading decisions. The use of additional indicators can also assist in separating great opportunities from the mundane. I wanted to illuminate the importance of relative strength, volume and breakouts in identifying outstanding trades, but also to have warned about the use of less proven methods that cause traders only confusion, and not insight.

But I didn't want to just write a book about technical analysis. There are many outstanding traders and investors who have scant regard for it, instead they rest their market opinion on the pillars of fundamental analysis and political developments, as well as economic and historical precedents. Many of these traders do very well and to restrict this book to technical analysis would be akin to looking at the market with one eye closed, artificially and unnecessarily restricting what is seen. Traders should develop a core trading system, but their circle of knowledge and the factors that they consider should be without defined circumference. A great trader thinks broadly, but expresses his well-informed opinion through an elegantly simple trading strategy, which utilises only a small number of primary indicators to know if the market is right for the proposed trade.

Another insight that I hope you will have noted is that great opportunities do not arise continuously. The type of trades that really put a notch on a trader's headboard occur once every 2-5 years and often present the potential to earn several hundred percent profit in just a few years. They typically occur following a period when a market has reached an extreme valuation. Catching the trends that emerge following these events can make traders seriously rich. Using the methodology outlined in this book will help you to identify these opportunities, and extract maximum profit from them.

My final, and probably most important point, is that successful trading is not just about knowing good strategies, it is about decision making. Decision making starts with doing a thorough analysis, much like the elite forecasters whose decision making skills we analysed. They examined a wide array of evidence from a myriad of perspectives, critically analysing its validity, relevance and reliability and only after this did they make a decision. But once a decision is made they continue to scrutinise it, looking for the hole in the boat, believing that nobody knows the ultimate truth, yet always searching for it. Many people believe that decision making can be taught by learning about trading psychology. Theoretical learning certainly helps, but only years of market experience can hone a trader's judgement to the finest of points. To that end I hope that the accounts of actual trades that feature in this book provided useful insight into the difficult decisions that a trader will face, and how to manage the challenge.

Thank you very much for reading this book, and I wish you every success in the future.

I would be most grateful if you would review this book on amazon.com, amazon.co.uk, or the website from which you purchased it. Many thanks, Jim.

One Final Thought

This book shows that using your tax free investment allowance to invest regularly in the stock market can produce exceptional results. I had a job that paid reasonably well, but with the expense of bringing up a young family I rarely managed to invest the full amount permitted into the stock market that would enjoy tax free returns. Despite this, the routine investment of a modest amount every year combined with strong trading performance soon accumulated a substantial sum. The use of spread betting (a type of leveraged trading) on financial markets to enhance returns also provided a powerful boost to performance. Furthermore, contrary to common perception it isn't necessary to be a full time trader to achieve large returns. Indeed, early on in my trading career, after an excellent period, I announced to a friend who worked at the spread betting brokerage I used that I was going to become a full time trader. He advised that it might not be a good move, and that he had witnessed many traders who became professional suffer a downturn in their performance. After feeling rather insulted, and wondering if he had actually seen my account, I came around to seeing his point of view.

He theorised that the pressure of having to make money caused a deterioration in trading performance. Unlike the Wall Street firms who charge a set percentage to manage a client's money, traders who become professionals and trade their own account enjoy no such income. Once they quit the day job they can become overly anxious not to miss trading opportunities, leading to bad decisions. I accepted his advice and kept the day job but worked only three days per week. During the stock market crash of 2008 and in several other instances the freedom of not being reliant on income from trading enabled me to execute larger trades at the most opportune moments, yielding much larger profits. Whilst others were scared of losing their shirts, I was willing to bet everything that the stock market would recover strongly. The wonderful freedom that private investors enjoy who have the knowledge and capability of taking their own decisions independent of other pressures is not a much talked about subject, yet it is vitally important.

The common perception is that professional traders hold all of the advantages, my experience shows something different. A trader with a mind that is free from the fog of pressure can trade with greater performance than professionals. I maintain income from other sources, including a small business and dividend income from my tax free stock market investment account. This enables a freedom to place very large trades at times of exceptional opportunity and helps to eliminate the pressure that can cause bad decisions. The advice provided by my stock broker friend not to become totally dependent on trading was of great value, and I am convinced it may be of value to other aspiring traders.

Glossary of Terms

A

Advance / Decline line a measure of market movements composed of the cumulative differences between stocks whose prices rose on the day and stocks whose price fell on the day.

Ask price the lowest price that a seller is willing to accept.

B

Bear a trader who has a pessimistic view of the market, expecting it to fall.

Bear market the name given to a market that has lost 20% or more of its value.

Beta this is the measure of how volatile a stock is. Higher beta stocks move more than the average stock. A stock with a Beta of 2 should be up 20% when the market is up 10%, or down 20% if the market is down 10%. A stock with a Beta of 3 should move by 3 times the market's move.

Bid price the bid is the highest current price that anyone is willing to pay at a particular time.

Bond yields the interest payment on a bond.

Bottom the low point(s) of a market movement before the trend reverses.

Break downward price moves that go below previous important low points of the trend, signalling that a new trend had formed.

breakout an upwards movement in price, when the price exceeds previous important high points of the trend. For example, when the price has traded in a narrow range but then trades at a higher price, signalling a breakout to a new uptrend.

Bull a trader who has an optimistic outlook who believes the market will move higher.

Bull market the name given to a market that has risen at least 20%.

C

Commission the fee charged by a broker for handling a trade.

Commodity a bulk product that is traded on the market, includes metals, foodstuffs or basic materials.

Consolidation after the market has moved in one direction it is common for the price to pause and to trade within a range to consolidate its gains before moving onwards in the same direction, hence the term consolidation.

Correction a significant price move lasting weeks to months when the price moves counter to the long term direction of the market.

Central Bank a national bank that provides financial and banking services for its country's government. It implements the government's monetary policy and issues the nation's currency.

Day trade a trade that is opened and closed within the same day.

Dividend cash returned to shareholders from the profits made from an investment.

E

Earnings per share the net profit earned by a company divided by the number of shares outstanding in the market.

Efficient markets theory a theory of markets that states the market price is a perfect reflection of all available information. The theory implies that markets price assets accurately.

F

Fundamental analysis   the study of the economy, businesses conditions and valuations to determine the appropriate price for an asset.

G

Growth stock   a company that expects earnings per share to increase at an above average rate.

H

Hedge   to control or delineate the risk on trade.

I

Inflation   a rising level of prices within an economy.

Insider   a person who has specific knowledge that shouldn't be known by traders.

Intermediate term trend   a price trend that has a duration of weeks to months.

L

Leverage   the use of borrowed capital to trade or invest with the aim of increasing the returns from an investment.

Leveraged Trading   the use of borrowed money to increase the size of a trade.

Long   a trade that will profit from the market moving higher.

Long-term trend   the direction the price has moved over a period of months or years.

Low   the lowest price the market traded at in a given time period.

M

Manipulation   the influencing of market prices by the use of non-standard methods with the aim of profiting from a price change, examples include the use of the media to issue stories that will influence the market price, or entering trades with the purpose of pushing the market in a particular direction.

Margin cash held in an account to fund trading activities.

Margin call the demand upon a customer to pay money into their account to fund trading activities, typically arises because losses have eroded the amount of cash in the account such that it no longer meets the minimum level required by the broker.

Macro trading a trading style focused on identifying large economic changes that have a national or global impact and then opening trades to benefit from the anticipated changes.

Momentum the underlying power behind an upward or downward price movement

Moving average the moving average is derived by calculating the average price over the time period

O

Offer the current lowest price to sell in the market.

Overbought the market is said to be overbought if it has exceeded the value justified by fundamental valuation methods or readings from technical analysis indicators.

Oversold the market has fallen further than is warranted by the fundamental outlook. Or, when speaking about a market being technically oversold it means that the market has fallen an excessive distance in too short a time. Traders who think a market is oversold expect the market to rise in the near term.

P

Price earnings ratio (P/E) the ratio of the current price of a stock divided by the annual earnings per share

Price earning gap (PEG) the ratio of the rate of earning growth to the P/E ratio

Program trading a trading strategy that is executed through a computer program

Pullback a short term price movement with a direction that is counter to the primary trend direction that the market is moving

Q

Quote the current bid and offer price for any traded investment or option

R

Rally a brisk rise in the market

Range the price range that a market has traded within in a given period of time, this can be the market's daily, weekly, monthly or yearly price range.

Resistance points in the markets history where significant trading has taken place and where attempts to move the market higher have failed

S

Short a trader who expects the market to fall and who has sold stock that they do not own, seeking to buy the stock back at a lower price, thereby earning a profit.

Short covering the process of buying back stock that has been sold short

Short position a trade to profit from falling prices

Short term trend a price trend lasting days to weeks

Stop order an order given to a broker to exit a position when the market reaches a particular level

Support a price level where prior falls in price have been meet with buying interest sufficient to abate the decline

T

Technical analysis a study of price and volume data to make forecasts about future price movements

Trading range a price range that a share price has been trading e.g. between 160-170p for 4 weeks. A trading range can last any length of time. Some trading ranges form over years others last only minutes.

V

Volume the number of shares or contracts on a given market that change ownership in a given time

Useful trading websites and blogs

www.moneyam.com   a U.K site that has free live streaming prices and an excellent charting package, as well as company specific information, news reports and bulletin boards.

www.advfn.com   has free streaming prices and a good charting package with plenty of company specific information and news reports

www.lse.co.uk contains a host of historical data and the latest news releases from the companies including annual reports, details about director shareholding all presented in an easy to use format.

https://uk.finance.yahoo.com/q?s=WPP.L   contains   analyst's estimates for almost every company listed on the stock market.

http://www.barchart.com/stocks/high.php a free list of stocks hitting new 52 week highs for the U.K, United States and Europe. Most sites charge for this information so this site is worth visiting.

www.scottgrannis.blogspot.com a great blog to help aspiring macro traders. The author uses relatively jargon free language and his blogs are readily comprehendible and to the point with a global relevance.

Thoughts from the Frontline a great weekly newsletter read by over 1 million people per week. An easy, yet informative read on economic, politics and finance with global relevance.

economistsview.typepad.com/timduy/ on central banking then this is an excellent blog. The articles are short and punchy, although sometimes technical.

www.bankofengland.co.uk it is always worth reading speeches by the governor and the deputy governor of the Bank of England. They provide a good overview of the U.K economy and the global economy. It is far better to read the actual speeches than rely on the media interpretation since the media emphasise certain aspects which can result in the trader receiving a distorted view of what was said.

Whichever country you live in it is always worth reading the speeches published by the central bank as they are very informative, accurate and relatively unbiased.

Website for the European Central Bank - the speeches by the governor and deputy governor provide a clear overview of the global economy and the risks and uncertainties that they foresee as well as an excellent insight into the European economy.

www.telegraph.co.uk/finance/comment/ambroseevans_pritchard/ this blog is written for a national newspaper in the U.K so it is a great starting point for novices to seeking to understanding economic issues, especially about the U.K economy. The articles are short, punchy, and interesting

http://krugman.blogs.nytimes.com/   economics blog written for a mainstream audience about macro-economic issues, although it is heavily slanted towards the audience in the United States.

NOTE : Exercise caution when reading economics blogs as the bloggers often have strongly defined political opinions that influence how they view the economy and policies that should be enacted.

Legal Disclaimer

The author shall not be liable for any losses whatsoever, including, but not limited to special, incidental, consequential, or other damages. Whilst the author and publisher have used their best efforts in preparing this book, they make no representations or warranties with respect to the accuracy or completeness of this book and specifically disclaim any implied warranty or fitness for particular purpose.

No warranty may be created or extended by sales representatives. The information and strategies contained herein may not be suitable for your situation. The author is an experienced trader and investor, but is not a qualified financial adviser. Therefore the contents of this book are not financial advice, they are trading strategies that the author has found to provide excellent results in the past. No warranty can be provided for their future performance.

This book is not a substitute for professional services. Seek professional financial advice where appropriate before making any type of investment decision. All types of trading and investment involve risk of significant loss or gain.

References

1. Darvas, N. (2011) *How I Made $2,000,000 in the Stock Market*. Martino Publishing. (This book is worth reading in its entirety as it contains a wealth of experience and information).

2. Bulkowski, T. (2005) *Encyclopedia of Chart Patterns*. Wiley Trading.

3. Gladwell, M. (2006). *Blink: The power of thinking without thinking*. Penguin.

4. Reinhart, C. Rogoff, K. (2011) *This Time Is Different: Eight centuries of financial folly*. Princeton University Press.

5. Michael Shermer, Patternicity : *Finding Meaningful Patterns In Meaningless Noise*. Scientific American, 1st December, 2008.

6. Stan Drunkenmiller, Delivering Alpha , 20 July, 2015.

Printed in Great Britain
by Amazon